C000029515

THE SUBTLE ART OF NOT GIVING A CROC!

THE SUBTLE ART OF NOT GIVING A CROC!

LEGENDARY FRONT PAGES FROM THE

VOLUME TWO

hachette
AUSTRALIA

Published in Australia and New Zealand in 2018
by Hachette Australia
(an imprint of Hachette Australia Pty Limited)
Level 17, 207 Kent Street, Sydney NSW 2000
www.hachette.com.au

10 9 8 7 6 5 4 3 2 1

Copyright © Nationwide News Pty Limited – NT Division 2018

This book is copyright. Apart from any fair dealing for the purposes of private study, research, criticism or review permitted under the *Copyright Act 1968,* no part may be stored or reproduced by any process without prior written permission. Enquiries should be made to the publisher.

A catalogue record for this
book is available from the
National Library of Australia

ISBN 978 0 7336 4184 8

Cover and internal design by Christabella Designs
Typesetting and internal layout by Isabel Staas and Kirby Jones
Printed in Australia by Blue Star Print

Hachette Australia's policy is to use papers that are natural, renewable and recyclable products and made from wood grown in sustainable forests. The logging and manufacturing processes are expected to conform to the environmental regulations of the country of origin.

CONTENTS

INTRODUCTION

FROM OUR MODEST BEGINNINGS, when we first rolled off the press in 1952 as a one-day-a-week paper, to a daily newspaper with a HUGE social media following and readership around the world, the *NT News* (and the *Sunday Territorian*) has come a long way.

From the very first edition we were determined to do things our way, the Territory way. Frank, fierce, funny and definitely not full of ourselves, after 66 years in the game we are proud that we are getting it right ... nearly 99.9% of the time. The little paper that could is now world famous for our headlines.

As far as we are concerned, the *NT News* is the best newspaper on the planet. (No, this is not being full of yourself. This is fact.)

Let's be frank, who else could have given you such gems as 'WHY I STUCK A CRACKER UP MY CLACKER', 'WHY I'VE GOT SOME STICKY NEAR MY DICKY' and 'WHY I STUCK A BUNGER IN MY BUNGHOLE'.

The answer is simple. No one!

But don't think we make those headlines up, they are built on genuine stories and they really did happen.

As we emphatically stated in our prime-time national appearance on *60 Minutes*, 'There is no fake news at the *NT News*.'

The Territory is as weird as it is wild.

Where else in the world would you find a transgender rooster, a bloke who used his rubber thongs as flaps on his beloved ute, a bloke who ate three coins at a Mitchell Street nightspot and a kangaroo trying to have sex with a pig? Gives a whole new meaning to the song 'I've Got You, Babe'.

This is life in the Territory and we bloody love it.

We love everything about the Top End. And we can list our three favourites:

CROCS. Crocodiles are a shining light in the Territory and responsible for contributing tens, maybe hundreds of millions of dollars each year to our tourism industry. It's estimated there are more than 100,000 crocs living wild in the Territory. Our human population is only 240,000. Crocs rule!

UFOS. The Northern Territory has also been a hotbed for alien and UFO activity. It's something we have embraced with genuine passion and enthusiasm. From legendary headlines about horny ghosts stalking women, to aliens doing crop circles, recent events have done little to quell any doubts that the truth is out there ...

SEX. At the *NT News*, we unashamedly love sex. Don't think we indulge in pornography (a staff member's mum did voice her disapproval, but she lives in the City of Churches so we just disregarded that). Perhaps we do cut close to the bone on the odd occasion, but only because that is what our readers tell us they want. The 'WHY I'VE GOT SOME STICKY NEAR MY DICKY' front page reached three million people on our own social media channels, making it our most popular in the digital age. The headline was the work of former Adelaide Crows footballer Ken McGregor and came about on a Sunday at a children's play café in suburban Darwin. *NB: Our team never rests when it comes to doing our best!*

BUT, while we are recognised around the world for our quirkiness, everyone in the Territory knows we're not just full of croc. As the Territory's main source of news and information we take our role very seriously on *all* topics. When we need to make a stand, we do it strongly.

When shocking vision of teenagers being abused at Territory detention facilities was broadcast on *Four Corners* in 2016, we didn't hesitate to run a front page with the headline 'SACK THE LOT OF THEM'. It was a story that stunned the nation and led to a Royal Commission being announced the next day. Our front page stance was revered around the nation.

Australian politicians were divided on the issue of same-sex marriage in 2017, leading to the implementation of a national postal vote. Our pollies may have been struggling with the issue but the *NT News* team didn't. We firmly believe in unqualified equality and we put that belief on the front page. We were the first newspaper in Australia to call for same-sex marriage in our headline 'DO IT NOW'. That front page reached more than 2.8 million people on our social media channels and earned us plaudits around the country and around the world. Everyone loves a plaudit or two, but we are happier that the majority of Australians agreed with us.

At the *NT News*, we are proud to shine a spotlight on issues that really matter. We can, and regularly do, call out bad behaviour, inequality and abuse.

Was it the Dalai Lama who said 'We all have light and dark inside us'? It might have been another great philosopher. Our receptionist thinks it was Sean Penn. Anyway, whoever it was, they are right. At the *NT News* we will never shy away from serious issues, but we will always celebrate the light. Never fear, clackers, crackers and, of course, crocs are here to stay!

Thanks for all your support!!!

HOLY
CROC-A-MOLE

IT'S not like you can't live in the Northern Territory if you have a phobia against giant man-eating salties, but it would be tough. They are everywhere, especially in the *NT News* office. Our philosophy is simple. We love crocs. It's in our DNA. Whether it's a monster croc jumping out of the water on the Adelaide River or the slightly gruesome but strangely mesmerising image of a wallaby getting devoured, if there's a good croc story in the Territory we'll have it — and we'll likely run it on the front page. Nothing sells better than a cracking croc story. As far as we are concerned, they're one of the most intriguing animals on the planet and they will have a life membership with us until eternity. Crocs and thongs, ain't that what the Territory is all about?

1

We're for *you*

YOUR VOICE IN THE TERRITORY

NT News

Tuesday, February 20, 2018

ntnews.com.au $1.60 Country Retail 70 cents extra Incl GST

SNAP, CRACKLE, HOP

Hangry croc's meat prey >> P9

Smaug the crocodile mid-feast on a wallaby at his residence in rural Darwin
Picture: ADAM BRITTON

Naked thieves swim in croc-infested waters to steal dinghy

BARE-ARSED BANDITS

WILL ZWAR

A BARE-ARSED bandit and his accomplice ignored the threat of crocodiles, box jellyfish and sharks to swim up to a dinghy and steal it from the Dinah Beach Yacht Club.

The two men were cap-
tured on CCTV swimming to the Tipperary Waters venue under the cover of darkness and clambering into the dinghy.

As the second man climbed into the boat his bare bum mooned the security camera.

↘ P2: FULL STORY

76TH ANNIVERSARY
THE BOMBING OF DARWIN REMEMBERED >> P4-5

YOUR VOICE IN THE TERRITORY

NT☆News

Saturday, August 20, 2016   ntnews.com.au $2.20 Country freight 50 cents extra Incl GST

GET YOUR FREE HOT CHIPS
COUPON >> P5

WE HELP FIND 5000 JOBS IN 50 DAYS
CAMPAIGN LAUNCH >> P12,13

realestate

FIND YOUR DREAM HOME
48-PAGE MAG >> INSIDE

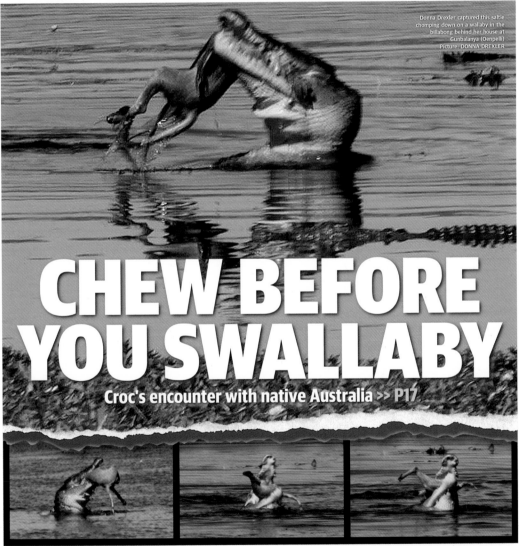

Donna Drexler captured this saltie chomping down on a wallaby in the billabong behind her house at Gunbalanya (Oenpelli)
Picture: DONNA DREXLER

CHEW BEFORE YOU SWALLABY

Croc's encounter with native Australia >> P17

LINDY CHAMBERLAIN REVEALS HER PERSONAL LETTERS 〉 **SATURDAY EXTRA**

Swallabied whole

By Maria Billias

POOR skippy never stood a chance.

When a 4m-plus monster comes hunting for an early dinner ... it's going to end in a bloodbath. And that is exactly what happened at Gunbalanya's town billabong on Wednesday afternoon when this fully grown wallaby was swallowed whole by the fiercest of predators.

And it wasn't pretty.

The images were captured late afternoon by budding photographer Donna Drexler as she and her partner sat on her back balcony which overlooks the billabong.

"We came home from work and were sitting on the balcony enjoying a cuppa, when I thought I saw a dead buffalo in the billabong," Ms Drexler said. "We got in the car and drove closer down the road to the billabong .. and we just saw this croc all of a sudden that flew out of the water.

"It had the wallaby in its mouth and it was thrashing its head side to side.

"Then he swallowed it whole. It took him about 30 seconds to do that. Nature is nature."

Ms Drexler, who has lived in Gunbalanya for seven months and in the Territory for 20 years, says this is the first time she has seen a crocodile so brazen in the wild.

"I've never seen anything like it.

"The croc was a monster. You can see in the photos there are other crocs around probably waiting to get in, but he was definitely the boss croc.

"I think when I saw what looked like the dead buffalo it was actually the crocodile drowning the wallaby at the time.

"It was a fully grown wallaby. It must have gone to the billabong to get a drink and was just at the wrong place at the wrong time."

The West Arnhem region is known for its monster crocodile population. Large crocodiles fighting over territory are often seen at the local Gunbalanya billabong, near Injalak Hill.

"Then he swallowed it whole ... it took him about 30 seconds ..."

DONNA DREXLER

Donna Drexler captured this saltwater crocodile chomping down on a wallaby in the billabong behind her house in Gunbalanya

Tuesday, August 22, 2017   ntnews.com.au $1.60 Country freight 50 cents extra   Incl GST

INSIDE TODAY NT☽News

YOUR VOICE IN THE TERRITORY

WHO WILL WIN?

2017 NT LOCAL GOVERNMENT ELECTIONS

Your complete guide to the Council that you're going
ELECTION DAY SATURDAY, AUGUST 26

GET YOUR FREE 32-PAGE COUNCIL ELECTION MAGAZINE

SWIM-BECILE

Reckless pop swims with crocs to impress the grandkids >> P2

This old fella risked his life by taking
a dip near an NT saltie trap
Picture: FACEBOOK

DRUG WARNING

Seven hospitalised amid a spike in synthetic marijuana use >> P2

VOTE 1
Simon NIBLOCK
LORD MAYOR and
LYONS WARD ALDERMAN

New Vision
New Direction

THE GREENS

Advertisement

Old fella has a reptile dysfunction

By Hayley Sorensen

THIS daft Territory grandad would do anything for love — including swimming dangerously close to a baited crocodile trap. The septuagenarian told the *NT News* he asked his wife to take the photograph to impress his 14 grandchildren.

"The idea was to send it back to the grandkids so they could think 'wow look at Grandpa'," he said. Unfortunately, the younger generation wasn't so impressed by his lunatic antics.

"I think they thought 'how silly is old Grandpa; he's lost it'."

The daredevil dill, who wanted to keep his identity under wraps, said he faced some nervy moments while he posed for the picture.

"I said to my wife: 'would you hurry up and press the so-and-so button', because she was taking her time," he said. But he said he didn't believe he was in mortal danger. He said other people had been swimming in the undisclosed location shortly before the picture was taken, though he admitted to becoming slightly more reckless with his life in his old age. "I had a really good look around for crocodiles before hand," he said.

"My grandchildren didn't think it was brave or courageous, they just thought 'Grandpa's lost his mind'."

Interfering with a crocodile trap can earn you a $70,000 fine, six months imprisonment or an extremely gruesome death. There have been 243 saltwater crocodiles captured in the NT this year.

LADIES' DAY 12-PAGE FORM GUIDE
>> INSIDE

NT'S BEST BUSINESS COVERAGE
>> STARTS P13

NT Business REVIEW
Door to $3 billion ship building contract open
All the news, all day, every day.

WHY WE'RE GONNA GET HOTTER
STORY >> P5

NT News

YOUR VOICE IN THE TERRITORY

Wednesday, July 19, 2017 · ntnews.com.au · $1.40 Country Freight 30 cents extra Incl GST

The croc at Cullen Bay yesterday and (inset) Tina Kievit and Chilli the dog
Picture: GLENN CAMPBELL

CROC STALKS CITY BEACH

Would you like a bit of saltie with your Chilli? >> P4

Darwin pony club to keep riding on

THE Fannie Bay Equestrian Club will likely live to see another 20 years, after a majority of Darwin Council aldermen threw their support behind the organisation.

Alderman Rebecca Want de Rowe will put forward a motion to next week's council meeting to extend the pony club's lease for another two decades. "I've always been supportive of (the club). I've met with the people and I've seen what a great job they do down there. It would be a huge loss to the community if the club was shut down," she said.

"Why would we get rid of them when we have no intention of doing anything with that space?"

The decision comes after council voted in July 2015 to cancel the lease in 2020, after little community consultation.

In June, the pony club delivered a petition to council to get the decision reversed.

❯ EXCLUSIVE DETAILS >> P2

Dying firey's inspiring pledge to family

TERRITORY firefighter Ryan Clay will never walk his daughters down the aisle.

On his 38th birthday in April, Mr Clay was told he had a stage four glioblastoma on his brain stem, and was given just a year to live.

The inoperable cancer will eventually take away Mr Clay's ability to use his limbs and damage his eyesight.

"Cancer treatment, and battling through that, is priority number one at the moment — that, and family," he said.

"Family — it gives you a reason to wake up in the morning, and reason to go home from work." With the time he has left, Mr Clay wants to do all he can to provide for his young family — and is determined to keep serving the community.

He joined the NT Fire and Rescue Service in 2004, and yesterday was presented with an Australian Fire Service Medal at Government House.

❯ INSPIRING STORY >> P3

LEGEND CAMERON ILETT CALLS TIME ON THUNDER ❯ SPORT

Peckish saltie lurking off popular city beach

By Molly Baxter

DOG owners partial to walking their canines along Cullen Bay Beach might want to give it a miss for a few days as authorities work to remove a pesky 2m croc spotted two days in a row.

It comes as rangers struggle to deal with the large number of croc removals following a bumper Wet, with 208 crocs dealt with so far.

The saltie was first seen by Cullen Bay mum Tina Kievit walking her dog Chilli on Monday morning about 8.30am. She said Chilli, a four-month-old Groodle, went to chase a seagull into the water before she spotted the croc and instead chased after it.

"The croc then began swimming towards Chilli and I was just screaming for her to get out of the water," Ms Kievit said.

"She wouldn't listen and the croc went straight into the water (after) Chilli ... and then I saw splashing and snapping.

"Eventually Chilli listened and came back to me so I just picked her up and walked (to safety).

"We realised the croc was still there, right off the rock wall, for the next hour."

But the very next day at the same time, the same croc was sunning itself in the shallows on the beach, a popular area for dog walkers and tourists alike.

"I think I will definitely be avoiding the beach down here for a while," Ms Kievit said. Department of Tourism and Culture acting director wildlife operations Tracey Duldig said rangers responded to the call straight away.

"It is difficult to catch crocodiles during the day as they are more likely to be submerged when approached by our boats," she said.

The site is being monitored by staff and signs have been put up at all entry points to the beach.

"Crocodiles are highly mobile and it is not unusual for them to be located in these areas," Ms Duldig said.

"It should be assumed that any water body in the saltwater crocodile's natural range in the NT may contain an animal and is therefore unsafe to swim in, unless signposted otherwise."

Melbourne tourists Ralph and Tina Braun said it was exciting to see the croc along Cullen Bay Beach yesterday, but thought there would be more hanging around from stories they've heard about the Territory.

Tina Kievit saw this croc (inset) yesterday while walking her dog Chilli at Cullen Bay Beach
Picture: GLENN CAMPBELL

Tuesday, January 23, 2018   ntnews.com.au $1.60 Country freight 50 cents extra Incl GST

NT News

YOUR VOICE IN THE TERRITORY

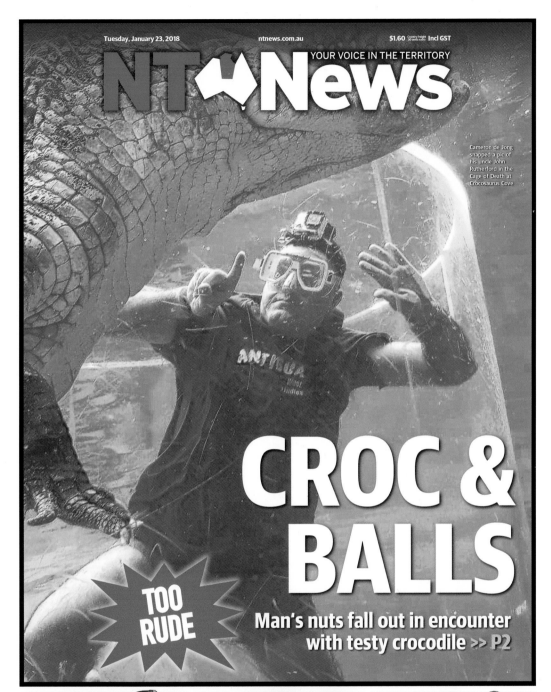

Cameron de Jong snapped a pic of his uncle John Rutherford in the Cage of Death at Crocosaurus Cove

CROC & BALLS

TOO RUDE

Man's nuts fall out in encounter with testy crocodile >> P2

GREAT AUSSIE DAY PIE EATING COMPETITION
STORY >> P3

OUR D'ARCY MAKES AUSSIE TEAM
>> SPORT

SPECIAL BACK TO SCHOOL FEATURE
>> SUNS NEWSPAPERS

Saltie nuts on show

By Jason Walls

THINGS got a little nutty at Crocosaurus Cove at the weekend, when a tourist swimming with the salties inadvertently put on a show of his own. Cameron De Jong was visiting Darwin with his uncle John Rutherford when he decided to surprise him with a visit to the popular tourist attraction. But the real shock would be reserved for those looking on.

"He was up here helping me with some stuff and I thought as a surprise I'd take him there and put him in a cage," Mr De Jong said.

"I got out the phone to get some photos and he started kicking his legs and I could see his bloody nuts."

Mr De Jong said he tried to get a message to his uncle from outside the tank but when that didn't work he decided to keep snapping away, knowing his uncle would see the funny side.

"I sort of pointed down to him but he didn't know what I was saying," he said.

"I thought I'll just take the photos, he'll get a kick out of it, he's a bit of a joker."

But if Mr De Jong was surprised at copping an eyeful from his uncle, it was another unsuspecting patron who was really stunned.

Mr De Jong said he didn't raise the alarm as it was a fairly quiet day at the Cove, but he couldn't prevent one lady from getting more of a show than she'd bargained for. "She walked up and she had a little girl with her and she said 'Hey come and look at the big croc and that man in the cage' and I thought 'Do I quickly say I probably wouldn't come over here?'," he said.

"His belly was right up against the glass and then the croc moved its tail and made my uncle a bit more visible in the cage.

"I could pick the moment she saw them because she said 'Oh darling, let's go look at a different croc'."

Mr De Jong said Mr Rutherford was able to see the funny side of the situation when he was finally able to let him know and wouldn't forget his trip to the Top End in a hurry.

"I thought 'I've gotta show him because he wants to see (the photos) and we couldn't stop laughing," he said.

"I think he's glad he did it now because he's got some memorable photos."

Cameron De Jong was snapping a few pictures of his uncle John Rutherford in the cage of death before realising John's testicles are exposed in the images   Picture: CAMERON DE JONG

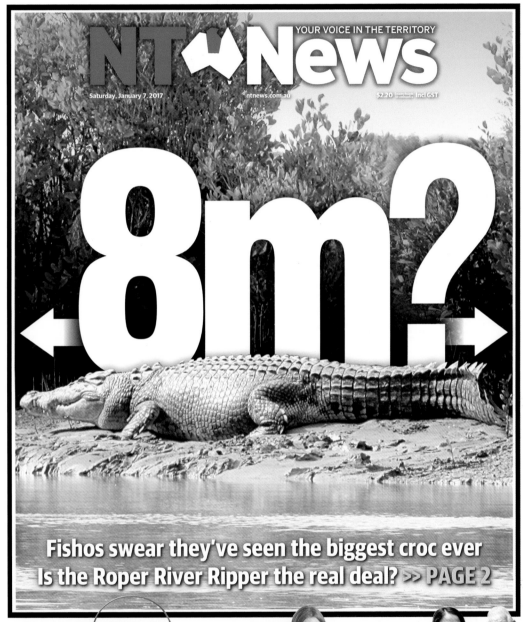

NT News

YOUR VOICE IN THE TERRITORY

Saturday, January 7, 2017 ntnews.com.au $2.20 Incl GST

8m?

Fishos swear they've seen the biggest croc ever
Is the Roper River Ripper the real deal? >> PAGE 2

ULTIMATE WET SEASON ACTIVITY BUCKET LIST
SATURDAY EXTRA >> INSIDE

WHY WE SHOULDN'T KEEP MUM ON ABORTION
JILL POULSEN >> P11

RAISING A GLASS FOR HIT AND RUN VICTIM
REPORT >> P9

Biggest croc ever seen?

By Molly Baxter

A MONSTER crocodile lurking in the deep, dark waters of the Roper River could be the biggest on record, with several fishermen claiming it to be at least 8m long.

The photo of the alleged 8m saltie was taken by Katherine man Richard Sallis and his mate Ian Graham, who were fishing along the Roper, about 300km from Katherine, near Black Fella Creek.

Mr Sallis said he spotted the croc along the bank of the river during the 2014 Dry season while they were in a 6.5m tinnie but he hasn't seen it since, or in the nine years before that he had been fishing at the same spot.

His claims of it being 8m were backed up by other fishermen, who measured it against their drag net.

The croc, now something of a Roper River legend, could be anywhere with the river spanning more than 1000km.

"We just couldn't believe our eyes," Mr Sallis said. "That's why there's no fish in the river, we couldn't catch anything because he's eaten it.

"A couple of guys said they saw him after us and physically measured him by their drag net and then they said 'you were right Richard, he was 8m'. "We were over the moon because it's a once in a lifetime visual thing, and to see it live — you've just got to be at the right place at the right time."

Mr Sallis said the croc had been in a few fights as he was missing some fins along his tail though there'd be no dispute that he now owns the river. "He was huge — it's the stuff of scary movies," he said.

"We cherish the picture we've got as he's King of the Roper, he'd still be around."

Crocodile expert Grahame Webb had his doubts that the croc truly was 8m long, as there was nothing to measure the prehistoric beast. "There's nothing to scale this photo to in the picture, nor to suggest why it would not be in the four to five metre range," he said.

"The head is really quite smooth where most of the really big, old crocodiles have all sorts of bumps along the snout.

"The only accurate way would have been to use the photo to put a stick in the mud near the tip of the snout, and another stick in the mud level with where the tail tip would have been and measure the straight-line distance."

The NT is famous for its monster crocs with Adelaide River giant Dominator estimated to be 6.1 metres in length and weighing over a ton. Cassius, a male saltwater crocodile caught in the Finniss River in the NT, is recognised as the world's largest crocodile in captivity at 5.48m in length, and weighing in at 968kg.

The Territory's own superstar Brutus, a neighbour of Dominator in the Adelaide River, is estimated to be around 5.5m.

The 8m Roper River Ripper in 2014
Picture: RICHARD SALLIS

BUREAU WARNS CYCLONE COULD BREW ON SUNDAY

STORY >> P3

EAT LOCAL SEAFOOD THIS CHRISTMAS

STORY >> P10

ST MARY'S GUN FOR ARCH RIVALS

>> JUST FOOTY LIFTOUT

YOUR VOICE IN THE TERRITORY

NT News

Friday, December 16, 2016   ntnews.com.au $1.40 Country freight 30 cents extra Incl GST

HUNGRY RAIDER'S HUGE BEEF

Problem croc relocated to resort after chomping on station's cattle >> P4

Outback Wrangler Matt Wright wrestles the huge croc

TRUE VALUE AT A DRIVE THROUGH NEAR YOU!

Pit Lane Liquor
2/3 Middleton St., Yarrawonga, NT 0830

BEACHFRONT HOTEL
342 Casuarina Drive, Rapid Creek, NT 0810

HDT
HUMPTY DOO TAVERN
Humpty Doo Shopping Centre, Humpty Doo, NT 0836

CARLTON DRY
LOWER CARBOHYDRATES · SMOOTH
Carlton Dry Cans/Stubbies 24pk
Carlton Dry Lime Stubbies 24pk
$44.99ea

Merry Christmas
3 Days Only!

$41.99ea

GREAT NORTHERN BREWING CO.
SUPER CRISP LAGER
Great Northern Stubbies 24pk

Retail Limits Apply. Offers Valid 16/12/16 until 18/12/16. Pit Lane Liquor Closed Sunday.

CASUARINA SQUARE IS OPEN 9AM - 9PM TODAY

Monster croc gets moved

By Ashley Manicaros

A 4.5-METRE crocodile originally captured for eating nearby station livestock has been relocated by the Outback Wrangler to new digs.

Dubbed "Two Dogs", the saltwater crocodile has been moved to Sandpalms Roadhouse into a purpose-built pen, about 100km from Darwin. It had been located at one of Matt Wright's operational bases.

Sandpalms owner Tommy Abdoo said the pen for the monster reptile was complete with shade and a viewing platform.

"I had wildlife officer Tommy Nichols come out and inspect the pen," Mr Abdoo said. "He said it was one of the best private pens he'd seen."

The reptile, estimated to weigh more than 500kg, was moved about 15km from where it was being held without incident.

Mr Abdoo said they drained its pond to expose it, then lassoed its nose before using a 4WD Polaris to drag the monster out of the water onto a trailer.

"He's a big boy, probably about 60 years old," Mr Abdoo said. "We've talked about moving him for a while but I wanted to build the pen. He was taking livestock at the Finniss River Station and a couple of dogs which is why they caught him in the first place.

"The operation went very smoothly. We got him off the trailer into the pen and he swam up one end then came back and had a nibble on the trailer light while we were taking it out."

Sandpalms is popular with fishermen looking at accessing the freshwater side of the Finniss and nearby Bynoe Harbour.

"The addition of a croc this size will add to the tourists who come here and stay for a few months during the year," Mr Abdoo said.

Mr Abdoo and his wife Julie bought the roadhouse seven years ago.

Outback wrangler Matt Wright (light blue shirt) relocates a 4.5m saltwater crocodile to Sandpalms Roadhouse for their new croc display
Picture: Supplied

COMMEMORATIVE TERRITORY DAY EDITION

NT News

INSIDE TODAY

Saturday, July 1, 2017 • ntnews.com.au • $1.40 Country freight 30 cents extra Incl GST

The Territory's Own Pauls MOCHA Iced Coffee NEW FLAVOUR

CROC WAR >> P4

FIREWORKS >> P5

UFOs >> P6

NEW FLAVOUR >> P3

CROC-KY HORROR PICTURE SHOW

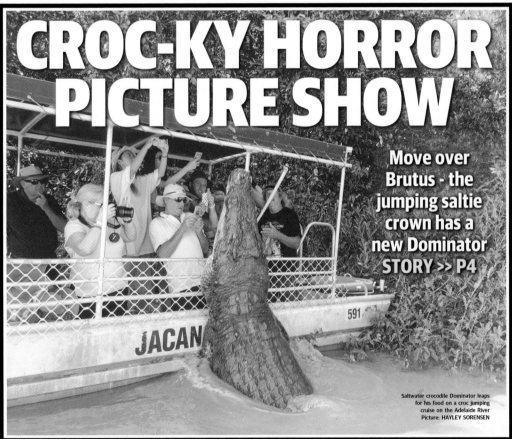

Move over Brutus - the jumping saltie crown has a new Dominator
STORY >> P4

JACAN

591

Saltwater crocodile Dominator leaps for his food on a croc jumping cruise on the Adelaide River
Picture: HAYLEY SORENSEN

Always wear your seatbelt.

ENOUGH'S ENOUGH. NT POLICE, FIRE & EMERGENCY SERVICES MACC ROAD SAFETY www.ntmacc.com.au

War of the crocs

By Craig Dunlop

HE'S long been the Boss Croc on his stretch of the Adelaide River, but now Dominator has put his name forward as being the Top End's most impressive jumping saltie.

Dominator — who measures somewhere between 5.5 and 6.1m — has been snapped leaping out of the water almost as high as the canopy of an Adelaide River Cruises tour boat.

The ferocious saltie lives just down the river from his world-famous 5m rival, Brutus, who himself shot to fame performing a similar feat on the front page of the *NT News* in 2011 under the headline "Yes, it's real". But the crocodiles' rivalry goes beyond putting on a show for tourists, with some believing a blood feud has developed between the two dominant males.

At some point over the wet season, Brutus — who has long been missing his front right arm — sustained a large flesh wound, which is yet to properly heal. Regular visitors to the area believe only Dominator could be responsible for Brutus' new battle scars, although Adelaide River Cruises co-owner Morgan Bowman believes it is more likely an outsider trying to muscle in to Brutus' patch who was responsible.

"Dominator doesn't like him, that's for sure, but we take care to keep them apart," Mr Bowman said.

"He's healing up well, but obviously it's going to take time ... we're very careful when we're feeding him not to do anything that might make his injuries worse."

He said the two legendary crocs had learnt to steer clear of each other over the years and respected each other's turf. Mr Bowman said it had been a busy dry season so far with both crocs regularly defying gravity for the sake of a piece of out-of-date meat.

"We let (the crocs) close, but not too close," he said. "Tourists, that's what people come up to see."

He said now was a great time to see the big fellas for yourself.

Saltwater crocodile Dominator leaps for his food on a croc jumping cruise on the Adelaide River   Picture: HAYLEY SORENSEN

NT☉News

YOUR VOICE IN THE TERRITORY

Monday, July 4, 2016   ntnews.com.au $1.30 Country freight 20 cents extra Incl GST

'RATS IN RANKS' HURT CLP CHANCES
STORY >> P5

WE NEED ABBOTT BACK IN CONTROL
ANDREW BOLT >> P11

CALLING ALL JUNIOR SUPER HEROES
DETAILS >> P6

Humpty Doo's Max and Pamela Tranter say they saw the infamous 9-metre saltie while fishing in the Norman River
Picture: ELISE DERWIN

REAL MONSTER

Territory couple adamant they've seen the legendary 9-metre croc
>> REPORT P2

RE-TEMPT YOUR TASTE BUDS AT

The Quarter

OPENING 6 JULY

OPEN DAILY 9AM - LATE

RESTAURANTS
KIDS PLAY
ENTERTAINMENT
CINEMA
FITNESS

Casuarina Square
by The GPT Group

casuarinasquare.com.au

GPT Property Management Pty Limited trading as part of The GPT Group

Tale of monster saltie no crock, couple claim

By Lauren Roberts

RUMOURS of a 9m long croc living in Queensland's Norman River have been met with fierce public scepticism.

But Humpty Doo locals Max and Pamela Tranter say the monstrous snapper is every inch as long as people claim.

"I'd say it was an easy 9m, if not more," Mr Tranter said.

"I was mesmerised – it was absolutely huge."

Almost 20 years ago, the couple were out on their 12-foot Pointer in an estuary off the Norman River when they saw the saltie. At first, Ms Tranter said she thought the croc was a log.

"I was on the bank, the tide was going one way and this thing was coming the other way – swimming against the tide," Ms Tranter said.

"And all of a sudden, the log lifted itself out of the water. My God, it was prehistoric."

About 18 months later, the couple were out fishing in the same tinny when they saw the croc for a second time.

It was swimming down the estuary towards the boat.

"The second time, it was in front of us, its head was wider than the tinny itself," Mr Tranter said. "We couldn't do anything if they flipped the boat over."

The croc swam under the tinny and reappeared behind the boat.

The couple would not reveal the exact spot they spotted the croc, afraid the snapper would be caught and killed if found.

"They'll kill it if they catch it," Mr Tranter said. "It'll be the biggest trophy of all."

Ms Tranter said she did not care if people didn't believe their story.

"We know we're telling the truth," she said.

This is thought to be a shot of the giant saltwater crocodile that stalks the Norman River

LOVE IN AIR FOR FRISKY FROGGIES
STORY >> P3

FESTIVAL DRAWS IN 60,000 PEOPLE
REPORT >> P9

TALLENT TO CARRY FLAG AS GAMES END
DETAILS >> P40

NT News

YOUR VOICE IN THE TERRITORY

AUSTRALIAN OLYMPIC TEAM PARTNER

Monday, August 22, 2016   ntnews.com.au $1.40 Country freight 30 cents extra Incl GST

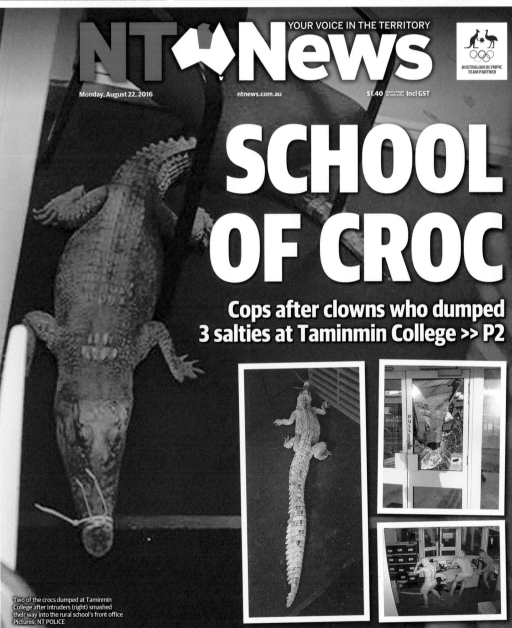

SCHOOL OF CROC

Cops after clowns who dumped 3 salties at Taminmin College >> P2

Two of the crocs dumped at Taminmin College after intruders (right) smashed their way into the rural school's front office
Pictures: NT POLICE

PACK OF WILD DOGS IN LITCHFIELD COUNCIL'S SIGHTS ⟩ P3

Crocs left at school in bizarre break-in

By Ashley Manicaros

THREE malnourished female saltwater crocodiles were found dumped at Taminmin College yesterday.

The intruders smashed their way into the rural school's front office about 30km south of Darwin leaving the unexpected packages.

The crocodiles ranged in size from 1.5m to 2m. It is an offence to interfere with crocodiles in the Northern Territory.

Security alarms alerted the live-in school caretaker to the break-in and police were notified of the incident just after 5am. The crocodiles, muzzled with garden ties, were in reasonable health but malnourished, according to wildlife officers.

Police Duty Superintendent Rob Burgoyne said forensics were examining evidence including CCTV footage.

"At about 5am yesterday the alarms went off at Taminmin high school," he said. "The front double doors had the glass panel smashed to gain entry and there was some damage inside the rooms. The caretaker who lives on site was the first to arrive and found the three female saltwater crocodiles inside. Wildlife rangers have got them and it appears they are healthy although slightly malnourished."

Police believe four people were part of the break-in. Stills taken from the CCTV cameras show the men shirtless with their faces obscured with what look like T-shirts.

They are pictured rummaging through desktop draws.

None of the images show the men carrying a crocodile.

Police were not aware of any other break-ins in the area. Strike Force Trident is now investigating the matter. Senior Constable David Gregory said police are appealing to the public for information as to the identity of the offenders.

If you have any information in relation to this incident please contact police on 131 444 or Crime Stoppers on 1800 333 000.

Just last month a Bees Creek family, less than 10km from Taminmin, found a crocodile in their bathroom.

The 1.7m saltwater crocodile was apparently dumped as a practical joke. It would have required two people to catch and tie it and was left in the home with its mouth tied, but limbs and eyes unrestrained.

Rangers warned pranksters that interfering with a crocodile is an offence.

ADD TO YOUR GREAT AUSTRALIAN STORYBOOK COLLECTION >> TOKEN P3

FREE INSIDE TODAY: TERRITORY HEALTH AND WELLNESS MAGAZINE

Friday, July 28, 2017   ntnews.com.au $1.60 Country freight 30 cents extra Incl GST

YOUR VOICE IN THE TERRITORY

NT News

A huge croc leaps from the water in the Adelaide River
Picture: LEX WILSON

YES, IT'S REAL 2

Is this croc set to become the new boss of Adelaide River? STORY >> P4

i return®
bottles, cans & cartons

NOW OPEN   www.i-return.com.au

10¢ for CONTAINERS

CONTAINER RECYCLING CENTRE

11 TANG ST, COCONUT GROVE

OPENING HOURS : Monday - Friday 8am to 5pm | Saturday 8am to 12pm | Sunday & Public Holidays CLOSED

CRITTERS

GONE TROPPO

TO live in the Territory you have to love critters. If you don't, you are in a bit of strife because they are everywhere. You can't escape them. Not even in the loo! At the *NT News* a cane toad squashed by a line marker, a chicken that doesn't know what sex it is, or a snake drinking a beer is front page gold. Crazy critter stories are our bread and butter (after UFOs and making fun of the recent ridiculous antics of world leaders) and we can't get enough of them. The Territory is blessed with some of the world's craziest animals and the subtle art of finding the right headline to match up with a cracker of a photo is something we are very proud to have perfected at the *NT News* and something those on the east coast have yet to master. You need to be bold, irreverent and not take yourself too seriously. We rest our case!

AUSTRALIAN OLYMPIC
TEAM PARTNER

NT News

YOUR VOICE IN THE TERRITORY

Thursday, August 18, 2016

ntnews.com.au

$1.40 Country freight 30 cents extra Incl GST

PALMO COUNCIL TO CHARGE FOR PARKING
STORY >> P3

POLICE ACADEMY STAR READY TO WOW

WINSLOW DELIVERS A MOUTHFUL
ENTERTAINMENT LIFTOUT >> P15

HAWKS SOAR OVER SIXERS

>> SPORT

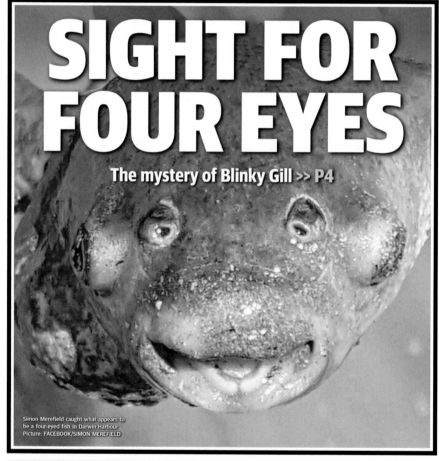

SIGHT FOR FOUR EYES

The mystery of Blinky Gill >> P4

Simon Merefield caught what appears to
be a four-eyed fish in Darwin Harbour
Picture: FACEBOOK/SIMON MEREFIELD

Mum's tears for slain Carlie

MARLENE Sinclair fought back tears as she recounted the last ever conversation she had with her daughter, Carlie, the night before she was allegedly murdered.

The last time Mrs Sinclair spoke to her daughter she was planning how she was going to tell her partner, Danny Deacon, she was leaving him, a court has heard.

Mrs Sinclair was called as a witness in Deacon's murder trial. Deacon, 45, has pleaded not guilty to murdering Ms Sinclair on or around June 18, 2013, at their decorative concreting business in Parap.

"She was sad, she wanted to move to Brisbane ... her relationship had broken down and she just wanted to get away," she said.
↘ **P5: FULL STORY**

Long Tan ban sparks outrage

THE Vietnamese government's decision to ban the 50th anniversary commemoration for the battle of Long Tan at the last minute is a "kick in the guts" and not the act of a friend, Veterans Affairs Minister Dan Tehan says.

There are now concerns about 1000 veterans who have travelled to Vietnam will be "shattered" after planning and paying for their trips.

The federal government is deeply disappointed and is representations at what it says is the highest level to have the ban of today's Veterans Day at the Long Tan cross site overturned.

Mr Tehan said the government was advised of the decision late on Tuesday without warning.
↘ **P2: FULL STORY**

A BOATLOAD OF FUN!

NT KENO

PLAY NT KENO FOR YOUR CHANCE TO WIN A $38,000 QUINTREX BOAT & $5,000 CASH!

EVERY $10 PURCHASE = 1 ENTRY TICKET

15TH AUGUST – 30TH SEPTEMBER 2016

Visit your local NT KENO venue for more details

Prize details: Quintrex 481 Top Ender S.C. with Yamaha F70 4 stroke motor, trailer & registration PLUS $5,000 cash!
Total Prize value = $43,487. Each venue draws a finalist on Friday 30th September at 8pm.
Major Draw on Friday 7th October at SKYCITY Darwin at 8pm. Terms & conditions apply.
Permit number HTL16/18. Please gamble responsibly.

skycitydarwin.com.au

NT News

YOUR VOICE IN THE TERRITORY

Thursday, November 17, 2016   ntnews.com.au $1.40 Country freight 30 cents extra   Incl GST

OUR ANDREA WINS NATIONAL AWARD

REPORT >> P7

LOW TIDE'S INCREDIBLE SPECTACLE

STORY >> P3

GET YOURSELF A CHEAP FEED

>> ENTERTAINMENT LIFTOUT INSIDE

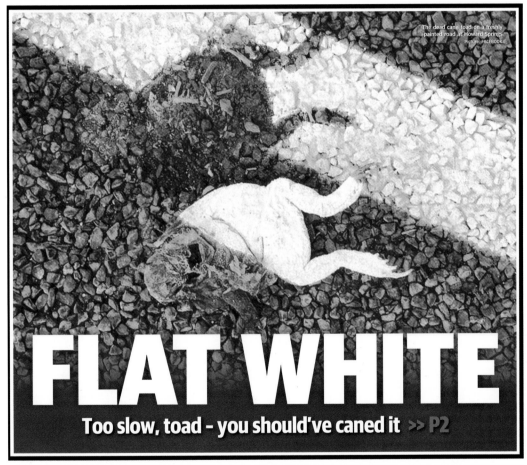

The dead cane toad on a freshly painted road at Howard Springs
Picture: FACEBOOK

FLAT WHITE

Too slow, toad - you should've caned it >> P2

All I Want for Christmas

Play Table Games for your chance to WIN a Toyota HiLux 4x4

SKYCITY DARWIN

PRIZE DRAW
9PM ON SATURDAY 24TH DECEMBER 2016

Terms & conditions apply. Permit number NTL16/36. Please gamble responsibly.

Art world left to ponder significance of dead toad

By Hayley Sorensen

COULD this oblate amphibian be a priceless work of art by guerilla graffiti artist Banksy?

Or did a linemarker just run over a squished toad?

We may never know the truth, but sources in the Darwin art fraternity said regardless of its origins, the piece made a powerful statement on the human condition.

One local artist interviewed by the *NT News* posited the theory that the installation, discovered by Stephen Boustead in Howard Springs' Corella Ave, was a metaphor for Australia's refugee policies.

"Here we see a foreigner who has come to this country seeking a safe haven, but has been viewed by those already living here as an evil and unwelcome invader," she opined.

"We as a society have painted it with a broad brushstroke and cast its mangled corpse aside to rot."

Reading deeper into the work's meaning, she said it could also be interpreted as a statement on the tension between the natural and manmade worlds.

The source said having a piece by an artist of Banksy's fame was a huge coup for the NT and could prove a tourist drawcard. The piece is on display now, and can be seen until the next time Litchfield Council repaints line markings.

Tony Gorell got a photo of a cane toad that had been painted over by a road line

NT News

YOUR VOICE IN THE TERRITORY

Thursday, June 1, 2017   ntnews.com.au $1.40 Country freight 30 cents extra Incl GST

LARGE CROAK AND HOPCORN, PLEASE

This juvenile python had its heart set on a froggy snack when it spotted this collection of hoppers out at Virginia on Tuesday

You won't believe what happened next ...
STORY >> P2

Tradies scheme's shock ending

ASHLEY MANICAROS

THE sudden ending of the Labor Government's successful home improvement scheme is to avoid oversubscription, industry sources say.

Acting Chief Minister Natasha Fyles was forced to confirm the tradies grant closure after the Housing Industry Association issued a press release yesterday morning expressing its remorse at the closure of the scheme and lauding how successful it had been. No new applications will be accepted after 5pm tomorrow. It is the second time the scheme has ended.

The scheme is ending because the allocated $15 million has nearly run out. All eligible applications that have been approved will be honoured.

Ms Fyles said the scheme has generated $60 million for the economy so far, and this was expected to increase once the $15 million was allocated.

↘ **Full story: P3**

Natasha Fyles

Gina's cattle plan for Darwin Port

GARY SHIPWAY

THE Territory's largest land owner, Gina Rinehart, is putting together major expansion plans for her growing cattle empire with the Darwin Port to have a key role.

The result would be a massive new live cattle trade to China doubling the size of Australia's current $1.5 billion live cattle industry.

It will potentially turn the Top End into a mass cattle yard from which livestock can be shipped to overseas buyers.

Ms Rinehart is not commenting, but she was in Shanghai two weeks ago for a Kidman and Co board meeting. While there she reportedly met with the Chinese government for talks about establishing a live cattle receivable area.

Ms Rinehart and Shanghai CRED Real Estate Stock Co spent $365 million last year to acquire S. Kidman and Co.

↘ **Full story: P5**

Gina Rinehart

Frogs escape snake's family meal deal plans

By Jill Poulsen

MOST loving parents would lay down their life for their children and it seems frog parents are no exception.

A Virginia local was relaxing on her patio around 7pm Tuesday evening when she saw a juvenile python heading towards a family of green tree frogs. She said she was touched by what she saw.

"It's like the big ones came out and said 'we're getting in front so you can't get our babies'," she said.

"It was really cute."

Miraculously all of the frogs survived the close encounter.

"Thankfully they were all still there in the morning," she said. "We've lived here for eight and a half years and they've (frogs) always been there."

It was only the second time they'd had a snake come so close to the house, though.

She said the "classic NT nature" moment was just one of the things she loved about living rural.

The Territorian's attitude is in stark contrast to the southerners who made headlines this week when they were labelled "adventure-averse" by Treasury Secretary John Fraser during a Senate economics committee.

He said a new generation of soft youngsters were thumbing their noses at living in the Top End.

"How sad it is that younger people in particular are not willing to have a bit of an adventure and spend time in Darwin," he said while outlining economic growth patterns in cities across the country.

Mr Fraser said Jodie Ryan, the head of the NT's public service, had asked for a Canberra public servant to come and work in Darwin for three months but not one of them wanted to take up the position.

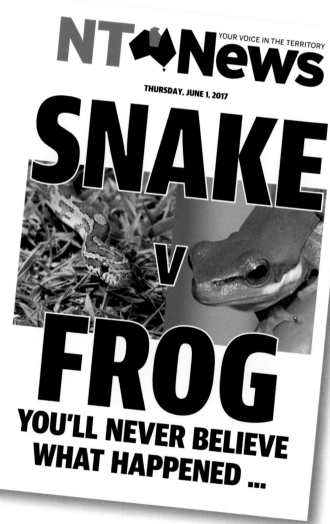

NT News
YOUR VOICE IN THE TERRITORY

THURSDAY, JUNE 1, 2017

SNAKE
v
FROG
YOU'LL NEVER BELIEVE WHAT HAPPENED ...

GET YOUR 24-PAGE 2018
ROYAL DARWIN SHOW GUIDE
LET THE FUN BEGIN
CELEBRATING THE YEAR OF THE DOG
>> INSIDE TODAY

COMPANY POWER BILLS SLASHED
NTBR >> STARTS P15

Business
REVIEW
Business benefiting from electricity battle

We're for *you*
YOUR VOICE IN THE TERRITORY
NT News

Hooster the transgender rooster scratches around at its Fannie Bay home
Picture: KERI MEGELUS

TRANS-HEN-DER

Darwin Show bound chook, who the *NT News* has dubbed Caitlyn Hen-ner, lives at Fannie Bay near Dick Ward Drive and is changing into a rooster >> P4

ADF love triangle trial

A JEALOUS feud between two groups of Australian soldiers was behind a violent clash at the Darwin Waterfront which left one of the men with a broken jaw, a court has heard.

Defence Force members Tory Staff, 24, and Colan Coleman, 20, pleaded not guilty yesterday to assault and causing serious harm. The pair are facing trial for the alleged attack on Army truck drivers Jordan Clark and Sean Hanson after last year's AFL Grand Final.

Staff's barrister, Jon Tippett QC, said there was "bad blood" between Mr Clark's group of friends and Mr Lowth's friends over separate relationships the men had with the same woman.
↘ P11: STORY

Open letter promise

TODAY, the *NT News* writes an open letter to the people charged with ensuring the safety of our children and that none of them suffer the same unimaginable cruelty as one Tennant Creek girl, aged 2, did earlier this year.

Since the incident, the *NT News* has launched an unrelenting campaign vowing not to give up on this girl, or any other children in danger of being exposed to such abhorrent cruelty.

Following the departure of the Prime Minister from Tennant Creek on Monday, we repeat this promise and pledge to keep those in power responsible by holding them to account until all Territory children are safe from harm.
↘ P7: READ THE LETTER

Hero diver's NT links

HERO anaesthetist and cave diver Dr Richard 'Harry' Harris, who recently helped rescue 12 boys and their soccer coach from a Thai cave, received his world-class training in Darwin.

National Critical Care and Trauma Response Centre executive officer Professor Len Notaras said Dr Harris did an Australian Medical Assistance Team course with them in 2013. "AUSMAT is a training program which is hosted in Darwin," Prof Notaras said.

Yesterday, Dr Harris was one of nine Australians involved in the Thai cave rescue to receive medals from Governor-General Sir Peter Cosgrove to honour their efforts.
↘ P6: STORY

Confusion most fowl as hen bends gender

By Natasha Emeck

THREE months ago Pam Hamil's hen Chook showed some odd signs of masculinity. Instead of laying eggs, Chook began crowing at the crack of dawn. Her legs became thick and rooster combs popped up on the top of her head.

Chook the hen became Hooster the rooster.

Mrs Hamil said the whole transition was a "freak act of nature" that left her scratching her head. She'll be exhibiting Hooster at the upcoming Royal Darwin Show.The transgender chicken will be on display with poultry in the Joe Yates Pavilion.

"For five years she's been a regular brown hen laying eggs in my backyard until one day I noticed she started looking pretty butch," Mrs Hamil said.

"She grew red rooster combs on the top of her head, wattles under the beak, thick legs and long tail feathers. I was thinking of entering her in the show this year but what category would you put her under? She doesn't look anything like a hen and she's certainly not a rooster, so we decided just to put her on display in the poultry section as something of interest for the public."

She said apparently spontaneous reversal can occur in hens when their ovary is damaged and can no longer produce the necessary levels of oestrogen.

It can also relate to flock dynamics since it primarily happens when there is only hens and the flock doesn't have a rooster, so one of the hens becomes one.

But after 25 years of being involved in the Royal Darwin Show, Mrs Hamil says she's not new to some of the bizarre things you can find there.

"I run the arts and craft section and last year I found a green tree frog that had been born with three legs in our hall. I ended up keeping him, he's at home in a glass aquarium. We call him Prince Ching because it's Prince Charming without the arm."

Hooster is not the first gender bending Territory pet. In 2016, the *NT News* reported Jiji the cat had changed sex after undergoing lifesaving surgery.

Hooster the transgender rooster was originally a female called Chook, and, inset, "Cat-Lyn" Jenner who also changed sex   Picture: KERI MEGELUS

Monday, May 29, 2017   ntnews.com.au $1.40 Incl GST

NT News

YOUR VOICE IN THE TERRITORY

FINAL DAYS

SPECIAL READER OFFER!

GET A **SAMSUNG GALAXY TABLET** WITH **NT NEWS+**

$450 WORTH OF VALUE*

ntnews.com.au/extra or call 1800 031 353

NT News

PRAWN CROC-TAIL

NT Government to consider a minimum price on Territory booze REPORT >> P2

FLOORED

MONSTER SNAKE FOUND IN LOO

Ranger called in to help siphon the python >> SSSSTORY, P2

COUNTDOWN TO ORIGIN

FREE TEAM POSTERS

PLUS: FOOTY FEVER IN MEGA 16-PAGE

MADMONDAY

LIFT-OUT >> INSIDE

SWEET RIDE
NT News car used to steal cakes in crime spree

REPORT >> P3

Firm finds real life constipation cure

By Craig Dunlop

A TWO-METRE long snake dubbed the "boa constructor" had to be removed from the dunnies at local building firm Sitzler last week, but not before giving one of the Territory's most powerful men the fright of his life.

It's the stuff of nightmares — when a routine trip to the loo turns into an encounter with a fully-grown water python, a species which has been spotted in the wild devouring freshwater crocs whole.

Sitzler Construction director Michael Sitzler, who last year ranked 44th on the *NT News* most powerful list, lifted the lid on every toilet-goer's gravest fear on Friday. Those in the office said their boss maintained his composure, despite the close call with the creature.

Sitzler employee Kristy Chatto said no one in the building knew at the time the fearsome snake was non-venomous.

She said Parks and Wildlife snake catchers were concerned the snake might slither out of reach down the s-bend, possibly returning later.

"They told us to keep an eye on it," she said.

When the snake catcher, coincidentally Ms Chatto's father-in-law, arrived, all but its head had disappeared from sight.

"He absolutely saved the day," she said.

The snake measured up at 2.2m, around average for a fully grown water python.

The Adelaide River floodplains are home to the densest population of water pythons in Australia. In the wild, the snakes usually ambush their prey when it comes to feed beside the water.

Parks and Wildlife figures show the species accounts for 13 per cent of all snakes removed from homes by government snake handlers each year. The species is known to occasionally inflict a painful, bloody bite when threatened.

The species typically crushes its prey, including rats, bandicoots and wallabies to death.

Wildlife ranger Ray Chatto wrangles the huge python found in a Berrimah dunny while business owner Michael Sitzler watches on

NT NEWS

...R VOICE IN THE TERRITORY

SATURDAY'S RACE FIELDS **ARE BACK** IN FRIDAY'S NT NEWS!

12-PAGE FORM GUIDE INSIDE ...each and every week

Alice Springs resident Amy Ravenhall was almost hit in the head by kangaroo testicles that fell from the sky
Photo: EMMA MURRAY

HIGH TACKLE

Kangaroo balls fall from sky and nearly hit woman in head >> P6

Marrakai residents forgotten in floods

JASON WALLS

MARRAKAI residents fear they have been forgotten by the NT Government after heavy rains left them cut off from supplies and services.

Karen Kershaw said the local progress association had been left to fend for the region alone after more than 400mm of rain fell in the past week.

"There's no help here now, the association's trying to get a boat or something so we can go and get groceries, the pub's running out of stuff, isn't there a government agency that helps people that are stuck in a flooded area?" she said.

"It looks like it's going to be about three weeks before this even clears so what do we do?"

A woman had to be evacuated from Marrakai by air due to the floodwaters.

↘ **REPORT: P12-13**

Council bid to move into Darwin mall

EXCLUSIVE
ASHLEY MANICAROS

DARWIN Council is looking at filling the vacant office void in the CBD, moving its library and customer service into the Smith St Mall, the *NT News* can reveal.

Lord Mayor Kon Vatskalis has asked chief executive officer Brendan Dowd to explore the costs associated with such a move before taking it to the rest of Council.

Mr Vatskalis confirmed the move was being looked at and comes a day after a Property Council of Australia report listed Darwin as having the highest office vacancy rates in the country for the third year in a row. "The library used to be on the first floor of the Paspalis Centrepoint building when I first came to Darwin," he said.

↘ **P4: FULL STORY**

WIN ONE OF 200 DOUBLE PASSES TO THE MOVIES 〉 P14

NT News

YOUR VOICE IN THE TERRITORY

Thursday, November 9, 2017 — ntnews.com.au — $1.60 Country freight 30 cents extra **Incl GST**

GET A GOOGLE HOME DEVICE WHEN YOU SIGN UP AS AN NT NEWS+ MEMBER*

*Conditions apply

STORY, DETAILS >> P2, P14

JACK PERIS MAKING WAVES DOWN SOUTH

>> SPORT

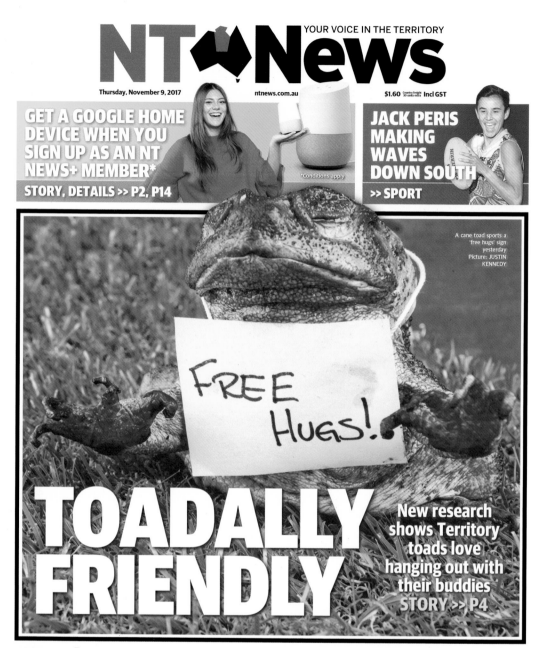

A cane toad sports a 'free hugs' sign yesterday. Picture: JUSTIN KENNEDY

FREE Hugs!

TOADALLY FRIENDLY

New research shows Territory toads love hanging out with their buddies STORY >> P4

NT's drowning concern

THE Territory still has the highest drowning rate per capita in Australia, says Royal Life Saving Water Safety Unit manager Jill Dowd.

"It's probably related around the outdoor lifestyles that we lead and the way we create and enjoy those activities around the water," she said. New data from Royal Life Saving shows 461 kids under the age of 5 have drowned in Australia in the past 15 years – an average of 31 deaths a year.

In the NT, 10 children aged 0-4 years have drowned, half of which were in home swimming pools. Ms Dowd said NT kids were exposed to water at a very young age due to the Territory's heat and outdoor lifestyle.

Ms Dowd said, considering how much time young Territorians spent in the water, it was important they learnt to swim and were supervised at all times.

⬃ P5: FULL STORY

Chinese flights on menu

CHINA'S Donghai Airlines has been in Darwin this week continuing talks with the Territory Government about direct flights from Darwin to Shenzhen.

Tourism Minister Lauren Moss would not confirm Donghai's presence in Darwin but a government source told the *NT News* the minister had a dinner meeting with airline executives on Monday night.

Donghai Airlines launched its first international route in September from its home-base Shenzhen with a service to Thailand's U-tapao airport. It is now eyeing Darwin. The Chinese Civil Aviation Administration announced in July that Donghai Airlines had applied for approval to fly direct to Darwin.

This approval had been granted and the airline had applied to Australia's Civil Aviation Authority for necessary approvals to fly to Darwin.

⬃ P3: FULL STORY

FRAUDSTERS TARGETING TOP END BUSINESS ❭ STORY P8

NT★News

YOUR VOICE IN THE TERRITORY

Monday, July 31, 2017   ntnews.com.au $1.60 Country freight 30 cents extra Incl GST

THERE WAS AN OLD LADY WHO SWALLOWED A MOZZIE

THERE WAS AN OLD LADY WHO SWALLOWED A MOZZIE

CONTINUE YOUR GREAT AUSTRALIAN STORYBOOK COLLECTION TODAY

ONLY $2.30 WITH TOKEN ON PAGE 4

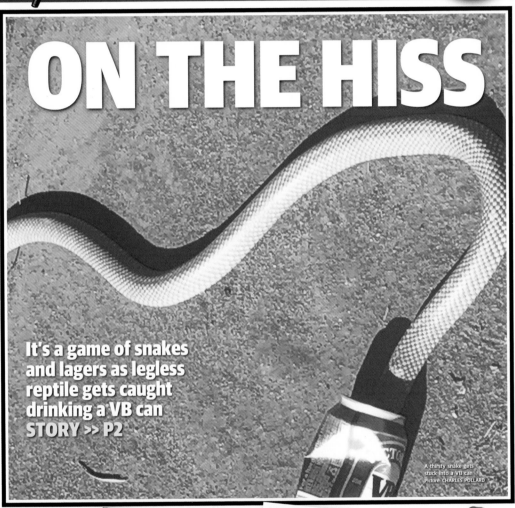

ON THE HISS

It's a game of snakes and lagers as legless reptile gets caught drinking a VB can
STORY >> P2

A thirsty snake gets stuck into a VB can
Picture: CHARLES POLLARD

THE DIANA LEGACY: PEOPLE'S PRINCESS
>> GLOSSY MAG INSIDE

SIX MONTHS ON AND NO SIGN OF REBECCA
SPECIAL REPORT >> P8-9

CROWS' GREAT ESCAPE AT THE MCG
>> MAD MONDAY

Boozy snake's legless after a day on the hiss

By Hayley Sorensen

TERRITORY coppers deal with boozed up and irate customers every day on the beat. But when two remote officers came across this legless boozer recently, they were sure to handle him with care.

The thirsty snake got itself stuck in a VB can and was unable to make its way back out.

Senior Aboriginal Police Officer Charles Pollard said the snake, thought to be a mulga, was in a foul mood when he and Sergeant Paul Wilson found it about 5km outside Ali Curung.

"He was alive and pretty aggro," he said.

With no wildlife services around, the officers tried to rescue the highly venomous snake themselves.

"We tried to get it off with a stick but we couldn't. We thought about killing it, but there was a family there so we said 'Righto, we'll let youse deal with it'," he said.

"He was a good size, probably just under a metre."

Rex Neindorf from the Alice Springs Reptile Centre said it wasn't uncommon for snakes to get stuck in discarded tinnies.

"When someone discards a can, generally they contain sugar so an insect will go in there, followed by a skink or a gecko, then a snake can smell that trail from the gecko," he said. "They go in there and when they try to get out, the can gets under their scales and they can't get out."

"If you see a can in the bush and can't take it with you, you should at least squash it."

A snake with its head stuck in a beer can   Picture: CHARLES POLLARD

NT  News

YOUR VOICE IN THE TERRITORY

Tuesday, July 12, 2016　　ntnews.com.au　　$1.30 Country Freight 20 cents ex10s　Incl GST

SPECIAL
80
PAGES

BRACE YOURSELVES FOR COLD, WET WEATHER
YES, IT'S JULY >> P7

12-PAGE DARWIN SHOW FEATURE
>> INSIDE

GET ON TOP OF YOUR FINANCES
MONEYSAVERHQ >> INSIDE

Power up your savings

Work the system to become a super millionaire

A wedge-tailed eagle
Picture: DAVID CAIRD

EAGLE TRIES TO STEAL BOY

Shock as dangerous bird attacks young tourist at show >> P2

ACES

STATE OF ORIGIN

WED 13 JULY 7PM

SKYCITY
DARWIN

skycitydarwin.com.au

PLAY STATE OF ORIGIN ROULETTE
$4000 CASH
MUST BE WON!

Purchase a schooner of XXXX Gold or VB to go in the draw.
Permit #NTL 16/18. *Terms & Conditions apply.

Nasty brush with eagle

By Jim Robertson

A WEDGE-tailed eagle performing in a popular Alice Springs Desert Park show tried to fly away with a terrified young boy, sitting in the crowd with his mum, according to witnesses.

Shocked onlookers at the park's drawcard Eagle Encounter show watched the bird swoop on the boy and latch on to his face and head with its talons.

"We were at the bird show in the afternoon having a great time and looking forward to seeing the wedge-tailed eagle come out for the finale," said witness Keenan Lucas, who was visiting Alice Springs from Victoria.

"The bird then flew over the crowd and tried to grab on to a young boy's head.

"He screamed, the mother was distraught, and the presenters wrapped up the show very quickly.

"It looked as if the bird tried to pick him up like a small animal and take off with him."

The boy, believed to be about six years old, apparently proved too heavy and escaped with just a gash to the face.

It is believed the boy and his family were visiting Alice Springs from Albury in NSW. The eagle has been stood down from the show. Mr Lucas said the boy was wearing a camouflage hoodie which had been zipped up to conceal his face — possibly confusing the bird.

"One thing I will say — is that staff handled the situation extremely well, and were calm and collected after the fact," he said.

With a wingspan of about 2.3m, the wedge-tailed eagle is Australia's largest bird of prey. The Alice Springs Desert Park issued a statement after the *NT News* contacted them about the incident.

"On Wednesday, July 6, an incident occurred at the Alice Springs Desert Park where an eagle made contact with an audience member," the statement read.

"A thorough investigation regarding the circumstances behind this incident is under way and the eagle will be removed from the show while this investigation is ongoing."

The statement said the boy suffered only superficial injuries.

Alice Springs Desert Park with a wedge-tailed eagle above

EIGHT-PAGE
DARWIN CUP
CARNIVAL
FEATURE
INSIDE >>

FRINGE
FESTIVAL'S
COLOURFUL
RETURN
ENTERTAINMENT GUIDE >>

FYLES FIRES
OFF AT
NORTH KOREA
NUKE THREAT
>> REPORT, P5

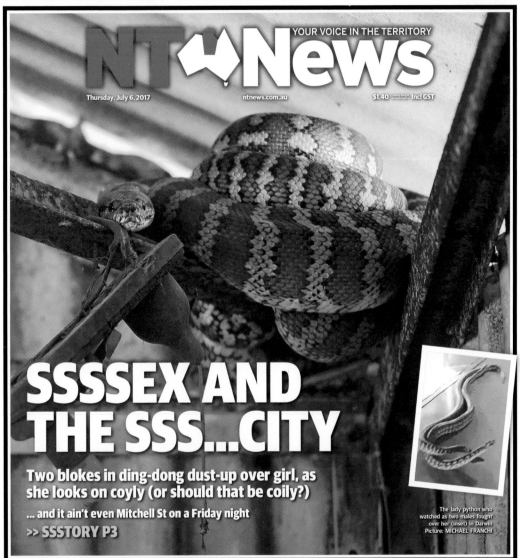

NT News

YOUR VOICE IN THE TERRITORY

Thursday, July 6, 2017   ntnews.com.au $1.40 Incl GST

SSSSEX AND THE SSS...CITY

Two blokes in ding-dong dust-up over girl, as she looks on coyly (or should that be coily?)

... and it ain't even Mitchell St on a Friday night

>> SSSTORY P3

The lady python who watched as two males fought over her (inset) in Darwin
Picture: MICHAEL FRANCHI

FLYING SHAME

Pressure on airlines as flight price rort hits new heights >> REPORTS, P8-9

Tangled love affair

By Hayley Sorensen

IT'S a scene that plays out in nightclubs and pubs across the Territory every night — two blokes locked in combat while a lady watches on, uninterested.

But the combatants in this fight for love were pythons and instead of Mitchell St, their arena was restaurant Pee Wee's at the Point.

Pee Wee's marketing manager Irma Miller said about 100 diners were captivated by the display, which took place at the restaurant's shed on Tuesday night.

"Every customer went into the shed; we were acting like tour guides," she said.

Tourists posed for pictures with the two pythons on the floor, while a third snake watched on from above in the shed's rafters.

"I'd never seen anything like it; it was magical and beautiful," Ms Miller said.

Warm weather is thought to have brought a surge in snake sightings and bites in the Top End.

Two men were flown to Royal Darwin Hospital on Tuesday after they were bitten by snakes in separate incidents.

In the first incident, a 52-year-old man was bitten at Florence Falls in Litchfield National Park around 10am.

Just hours later, a 49-year-old man was treated at the Batchelor clinic after he was bitten on the left hand by a snake he said was a taipan.

The taipan is one of the world's most venomous snakes.

Tom Parkin from Darwin Snake Catchers said there had been a clear surge in snake activity this week.

"It has definitely picked up in the last few days which is kind of weird because normally it's a bit cooler this time of year," he said.

"It might have something to do with the bigger Wet season we had. "It might be because there are more males around looking for females."

Mr Parkin said his team was fielding about four extra callouts a day. He said snakes were generally more chilled out in the Dry season months.

"It varies, but the period just after the Wet is when they're normally most active. That's when we see a spike in the number of snake bites."

NT🦘News

YOUR VOICE IN THE TERRITORY

Friday, June 10, 2016   ntnews.com.au   **$1.30** Country freight 50 cents extra **Incl GST**

STEVEN MOTLOP SPEAKS OUT ON FORM AND FUTURE

>> JUST FOOTY LIFTOUT

WHERE'S THE LOVE FOR OUR KAKADU?

STORY >> P5

I'VE GOT ROO, BABE

Outback kangaroo is hot to trotter for Apples the pig
>> STORY, PICTURES P8-9

TOO RUDE!

Apples the pig and this kangaroo are madly in love in outback Northern Territory. Their relationship has gone to a new level in recent times. Picture: RYAN FRAZER

DOWLING CELLARS

offers valid until 13/06/2016

Winnellie Cellars 📘📷
20 Benison Rd • 8984 3622
Howard Springs Tavern 📘
280 Whitewood Rd • 8983 1463

$19.98 10 pack   EARN $4 CAMEL CASH
Strongbow Cider Clear 10 x 375ml Cans
Strongbow Cider Original 10 x 375ml Cans

$46.98 each   EARN $4 CAMEL CASH
Great Northern 30 x 375ml Cans

$47.98 each   EARN $4 CAMEL CASH
PURE BLONDE
Pure Blonde 24 x 355ml Stubbies, 24 x 375ml Cans

$46.98 each   EARN $4 CAMEL CASH
CARLTON DRY
Carlton Dry 24 x 375ml Cans, 24 x 355ml Stubbies
Carlton Dry and Lime 24 x 355ml Stubbies

ORGANIC & PRESERVATIVE FREE WINES NOW AVAILABLE AT WINNELLIE CELLARS

Get some hot pork on your fork

By Craig Dunlop

A KANGAROO and a pig have struck up an intense romantic relationship in the tiny wayside town of Aileron. The animals' owner Greg Dick said tourists were often taken aback at the sight of the kangaroo — named "F**k It" — mounting Apples the pig by the side of the road. But he says he's powerless to intervene in the outback love affair.

"It's quite an unusual thing," he said.

"I tried to take the pig away the other day and the kangaroo nearly tore the fence down."

Mr Dick introduced Apples a year ago and said it was "love at first sight". "It just happened on the first day," he said. But despite being a gentle lover, he said F**k It was sometimes unfaithful. "He'll try to (get on to) anything, it's a wonder he hasn't had a go at the geese," he said.

Visitor Ryan Frazer was one of many tourists shocked by the sight of a kangaroo and a pig expressing their animal instincts with each other. On a recent work trip, he and two colleagues stopped in at Aileron, not knowing what there was to see.

"We were a bit stunned, I was with my boss and it was a bit awkward," he said. "They were nudging each other then he mounted her.

"Then when the pig mounted the kangaroo ... I've never seen anything like it." He said the presence of two geese in the paddock "just having a bit of a look" made the surreal situation even stranger.

"(One of my colleagues) was visiting from North America, it was definitely a memory he'll take with him, I'm not sure if that's a good thing or not."

Mr Frazer said Aileron locals commented to him that the once aggressive kangaroo became calmer when the pig came into his life. Mr Dick said F**k It showed no signs of leaving town now that he had a lover.

"If I leave the gate open, he just comes and sleeps on my veranda," he said.

Mr Dick said he couldn't bring himself to separate F**k It and Apples. "They're in love," he said.

He said the two animals had become an unlikely tourist attraction. "I think I might take some photos and get some postcards made," he said.

STEP ONE START OUT WITH A DATE... A SIMPLE STROLL PERHAPS?

STEP TWO THINGS SEEM TO BE GOING WELL... RUB THE PORK A LITTLE TO MAKE IT TENDER

STEP THREE EVERYTHING IS PROGRESSING AS PLANNED... HOW ABOUT SOME LIGHT PETTING?

STEP FOUR YOUR BACON SEEMS TO BE SIZZLING NICELY... NOW MAKE SURE THE COAST IS CLEAR

STEP FIVE JUST IGNORE THE HUMAN WITH THE CAMERA AND TRY THE PORK...
TOO RUDE!

TOO RUDE!
STEP SIX NOW SWITCH!!!

Pictures: RYAN FRAZER

MAMMALS OF THE SEA FEATURE
>> P16-17

INDIGENOUS BASKETBALL SETBACK
>> SPORT

WE'RE NOT EATING ENOUGH VEG
STORY >> P3

WOW!

Teen fisho lands 127cm monster barra 'Goliath' at Shady Camp >> P4

Tyrone Kollman with his prized catch
Picture: SUPPLIED

Demand for mangoes tipped to rise

TERRITORY mango farmers could benefit from the horrific weather smashing Queensland crops — but consumers might suffer — experts say.

NT Farmers industry development manager Greg Owens said farmers might experience an increase in demand this year after Cyclone Debbie and subsequent flooding destroyed produce in Queensland.

Mr Owens said producers might have to supply more fruit this season, but it was not yet clear if damaged crops in Bowen would make a full recovery before the start of the season.

"It's too early to tell on crops like mangoes," he said.

"They're so unpredictable."

Mr Owens said he didn't think Territory consumers would feel a noticeable impact on their wallets, but could not rule out price hikes.

➤ FULL STORY: P9

Mangoes are a hit in the NT

$1b pipeline simply not viable: Jemena

A $1 BILLION north-south gas connection is not commercially viable, Northern Gas Pipeline constructor Jemena says.

Independent South Australian Senator Nick Xenophon got the Turnbull Government to agree to a feasibility of the project in exchange for his vote on company tax changes last week. Jemena won a competitive bid process to construct the 622km NGP between Ten-nant Creek and Mt Isa in Queensland. "A gas pipeline from the Northern Territory to South Australia simply doesn't add up and is unwarranted," a Jemena spokesman said.

Lingiari MP Warren Snowdon condemned Senator Xenophon for not consulting the NT Government and "doing a dirty deal" over the Turnbull Government's tax cuts to business.

➤ FULL STORY: P3

Warren Snowdon isn't happy

OFF THE
DEEP END

NT News journos take their work very seriously. They're never off the clock. Pubs, parties, doctors' surgeries, pubs (did we already say that?) you never know where the next big scoop is coming from. When we heard about a bloke eating three coins at a bar we immediately thought it was a front page story. Not only did we get the story, we managed to get the X-ray vision of the coins near his groin which took it from a 99% likely front page to one of our best of all time. The headline WHY I'VE GOT A COIN IN MY GROIN was seen by thousands of people on social media. People in the Territory do weird things. It's just what we do.

NT News

YOUR VOICE IN THE TERRITORY

Friday, July 22, 2016   ntnews.com.au $1.40 Country freight 30 cents extra Incl GST

Michelle Fidock's dentures fell out into a commercial toaster at SkyCity Casino.
Picture: IVAN RACHMAN

Darwin woman reveals all on her buffet breakfast chompers horror story >> P2

TOASTER MELTED MY DENTURES

SHOWBAGS, SLUSHIES, DAGWOOD DOGS
SHOW ACTION >> P8,9

LATEST AFL, NRL TEAMS & NEWS
JUST FOOTY >> P19

BUY THE PAPER FOR CHANCE TO WIN $2370
>> BACK PAGE

There goes me teeth

By Maria Billias

THE story has become an urban legend — a set of rogue teeth flying into the toaster and melting on a bustling Darwin buffet breakfast table.

For a decade it has been occasionally spoken about and quickly dismissed as an old wives' tale.

But the nightmarish story is true. It occurred in 2005 at a SkyCity Casino girls' breakfast brunch, in a restaurant packed to the brim with V8 Supercar drivers.

For long-time Territorian Michelle Fidock, the incident has been a source of humiliation, pain and silence.

It has taken her 11 years to tell the story publicly.

The story dates back to 2005 when Ms Fidock, who has worn dentures since she was 12 following an ice-skating accident, lost her dentures after attempting to blow out a fire in a toaster at the Casino buffet.

What was supposed to be a quiet breakfast with her daughters Bianca and Jessica, turned out to be one of the more entertaining stories she would go on to tell — only close friends — for the next decade.

"We had finished breakfast and I decided I would like a cup of tea and a croissant," Ms Fidock said.

"So I cut it in half and put it on the wire rack on those toasters that rotate around .. and as soon as it hit the heat it caught on fire.

"So I tried to blow it out - and I went like that (makes blowing expression) and my teeth flew, not just fell, flew out into the toaster and started going around with the croissant that was on fire.

Bianca had the sense to run up and turn the toaster off and get the flames out, but we still needed to get my teeth out and we couldn't do it with the large tongs there.

So Bianca asked the waiter if it was possible to have any normal tongs as 'my mum's teeth are in the toaster and we can't get them out'."

Ms Fidock said what ensued after that — as the dentures had slowly melted away — was the hilarity of trying to retrieve them from the bottom tray of the toaster through the grates.

"We actually disassembled the rack but they kept falling down lower," she said.

"When we eventually got them out I waited for them to cool down, as melted as they were, and tried to put them back in. But they were so hot they burnt the top of my palette."

Ms Fidock said she had decided to tell the yarn publicly at the encouragement of her Nightcliff dentist Dr Steven Burlinson, who has since provided her with steel plate dentures.

"It's a belly laugh story now," Ms Fidock laughs.

"But for a while every time we went away to stay in a hotel, if there was one of those toasters there I would take a photo of it and send it to my daughters and go 'look who I'm having breakfast with'."

Ms Fidock said it was as embarrassing as the time her dentures fell out when she got food poisoning as a 17-year-old on a date with her now-husband.

YOUR VOICE IN THE TERRITORY

NT News

Thursday, February 2, 2017   ntnews.com.au $1.40 Incl GST

Peter Rogers has been using double pluggers as mud flaps and he bloody loves them
Picture: IVAN RACHMAN

CU IN THE NT

CHECK OUT MY FLAPS

Rubbery invention: "The old mudflaps on my ute were rooted"
THONGY STYLE >> P2

High-profile police trial looming

POLICE Commissioner Reece Kershaw and Corrections boss Mark Payne will be called to give evidence in the trial of their predecessor — sacked police commissioner John McRoberts.

Mr Kershaw and Mr Payne were two of three rotating deputy commissioners under McRoberts when he was removed as the NT's top cop.

The pair are among 14 witnesses from the government, political and legal world including former Police Minister Peter Chandler and Director of Public Prosecutions Jack Karczewski QC, who will take the stand during the hearing.

They are to be called to give evidence on the allegations McRoberts perverted the course of justice during a police investigation into disgraced travel agent and former Crime Stoppers chair Xana Kamitsis.

↘ **P4: FULL STORY**

John McRoberts

Daly open for barramundi fishing

WITH one month to go, keen Territory anglers could be one step closer to reeling in the million dollar fish.

One of the Territory's most popular barra fishing spots — Daly River Fish Management Zone — reopened for barramundi fishing yesterday for the first time since October 2016.

Amateur Fishermen's Association of the Northern Territory president Warren de With said the Top End's most lucrative fish could have been hidden all wet season.

"Everybody is interested when (the Daly River Fish Management Zone) opens up," he said.

"Lots of people will be heading down ... The whole Daly itself is very popular."

Mr de With said the Daly River was one of the NT's "most iconic river systems".

↘ **P5: FULL STORY**

The barra will be biting

Ain't nothin' thong here

By Hayley Sorensen and Molly Baxter

THERE are few moments in life sadder than a plugger blowout.

But one innovative Territorian has turned one of life's great tragedies into a wonder of bush engineering. Peter "Pedro" Rogers didn't know exactly what he would end up using his discarded thongs for when he began collecting his cast offs in the shed of his Darwin River home two years ago.

But he knew it was a commodity too precious to be thrown away.

There they sat, gone but never forgotten, until he had the brainwave that would give them new life.

"The old mudflaps on my ute were rooted. I needed something to replace them before the cops saw me," he said.

His out of service footwear had the perfect proportions. He bolted three old pairs to his wheel wells and has enjoyed life mud free ever since.

Although it's not the first time he's used thongs for the same purpose.

"They've been reliable but I had them on my old car, down at Kununurra, so thought I'd put them back on." As well as protecting his vehicle and passers-by from debris, the thongflaps are an excellent talking point at his Berry Springs Tavern local.

"Everyone down at the pub loves them," Mr Rogers said.

"People driving past always give me a good look and a bit of a wave and a thumbs up.

"It's recycling at its best."

Peter Rogers has been using double pluggers as mud guards
Picture: IVAN RACHMAN

EDITORIAL
NT News

No flip-floppin' on thong love

IN all the world, out of all the inventions ever created by the hand of humans, there surely isn't a more important tool for Territorians than the humble thong.

Call them what you will; pluggers, flip-flops or jandals if you're from across the ditch, there's nothing more necessary to live life in the tropical top of Australia than these rubber beauties.

Take, for example, if it's a day hotter than Satan's sauna and you need to walk up the shops for something standard for breakfast, like, say, an iced coffee and a carton of Winfield Reds.

You don't want your bare feet to melt into the molten asphalt.

But equally, you can't bare the misery of trapping your tootsies inside the sweaty, stifling caverns of closed shoes.

So what? Free your toes and walk the streets in peace wearing your pair of pluggers like a living legend.

But don't stop there. There's nothing one can't use a thong for.

That's why we love the genius invention of a typical thong-loving Territorian who, scientifically putting it, knew his "mudflaps on my ute were rooted" and so decided to replace them with a few spare you-know-whats. Now that's useful.

Peter 'Pedro' Roberts from Darwin River didn't lay down and cry like a bawling baby about the loss of his obviously much-loved mudflaps from his vehicle.

The Berry Springs Tavern regular used pure rural Darwin ingenuity and hooked up some discarded pluggers to fill the gap.

There's now even a name coined for them — thongflaps.

This is exactly the kind-of know-how Prime Minister Malcolm Turnbull has been harping on about in his mantra of "innovation" needed to help build the future of this great land.

The world's eyes should now be firmly focused on Pedro, his ute, his thongs, and what amazing idea he'll come up with next.

NT★News

YOUR VOICE IN THE TERRITORY

Friday, June 23, 2017   ntnews.com.au $1.40 Country freight 30 cents extra Incl GST

32-PAGE 4WD, BOATING AND CAMPING EXPO MAGAZINE
>> INSIDE TODAY

GET A SAMSUNG TABLET WHEN YOU BECOME AN NT NEWS+ MEMBER
LIMITED TIME ONLY OFFER >> P14

Anula pensioner Michael Woodhams has figured out we're getting ripped off for toilet paper Picture: MICHAEL FRANCHI

RIPPED OFF

Darwin pensioner claims he's unravelled toilet paper scandal >> P8

Cab drivers threaten to walk off the job tonight amid police defect blitz >> P6

TAXI STRIKE

SUPERBOOT 'BOOF' CELEBRATES 700 BIG ONES
JUST FOOTY LIFTOUT >> INSIDE

Territory man exposes nationwide bog paper scandal

By Tamara Howie

FIRST it was chip packets. Then it was chocolate bars. Now it's toilet paper.

Companies reducing the size of products but not the price has been around for years. And one observant Darwinite has discovered Australians are getting a crappy deal with bog rolls.

Anula pensioner Michael Woodhams, 75, noticed the Woolworths home brand toilet paper had reduced their sheet size from 11cm x 10cm to 10.5cm x 10cm. The decrease equals 130cm per roll, or 11 fewer sheets, which means consumers are missing out on about one roll per 24 pack.

"They don't realise it's going to be one roll less (in a 24 pack). They probably wouldn't notice it — but I don't know how people use toilet paper," he said.

Mr Woodhams — who buys toilet paper in bulk — said there was just a .05 cent price drop from $3.69 to $3.65 per 12 pack, which is just a 1.08 per cent price reduction despite the 4.54 per cent size reduction.

"I'll keep using it, it's the cheapest around," he said.

A Woolworths spokesman said the supermarket's "toilet paper options are high quality and excellent value".

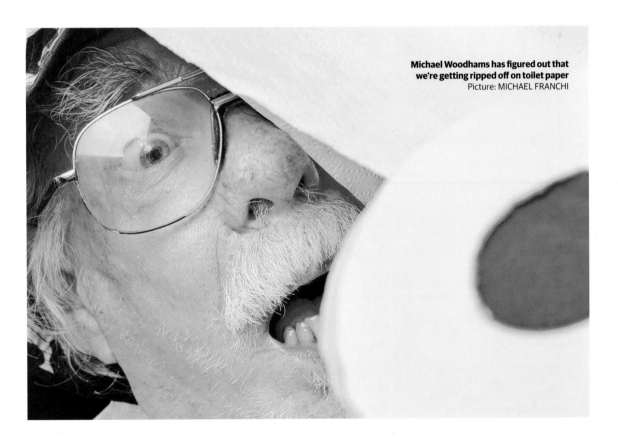

Michael Woodhams has figured out that we're getting ripped off on toilet paper
Picture: MICHAEL FRANCHI

YOUR VOICE IN THE TERRITORY

NT News

Wednesday, September 10, 2014 ntnews.com.au $1.20 Country freight 50 cents extra Incl GST

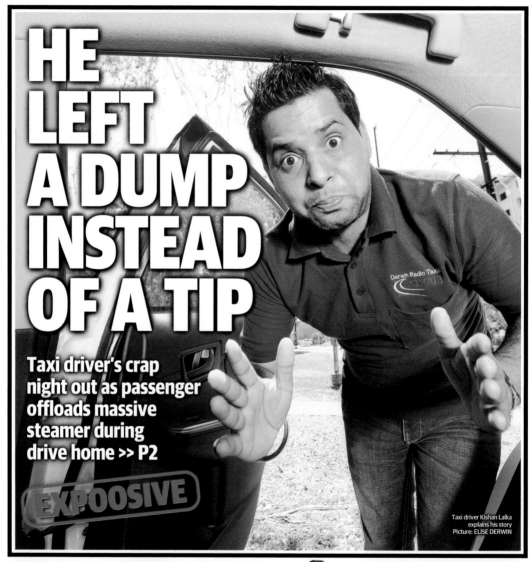

HE LEFT A DUMP INSTEAD OF A TIP

Taxi driver's crap night out as passenger offloads massive steamer during drive home >> P2

EXPOOSIVE

Taxi driver Kishan Lalka
explains his story
Picture: ELISE DERWIN

MAN ARRESTED OVER CITY DEATH
STORY >> P5

OUTRAGEOUS CELEBRITY DIVA DEMANDS
REVEALED >> P30

WIN TICKETS TO THE AFL GRAND FINAL
DETAILS >> P42

Cabbie's crappy fare

By Conor Byrne

TAXI driver Kishan Lalka knew his career would never be the same when he heard his passengers sniggering, the sound of pants being hastily buttoned, and a particularly pungent aroma filling his nostrils.

The 30-year-old Darwin Radio Taxis driver had picked up five passengers in his VW Caddy maxi taxi outside the old Honeypot strip club on Darwin's Mitchell St at 9.30pm on Monday.

It seemed a normal fare, then things went terribly wrong.

"One guy who was sitting on the behind seat, he did the worst s--- — (it) can't even be imagined by a human being," Mr Lalka told the *NT News*.

The boys had asked to be dropped off at Bayview St in Fannie Bay. He said they were drunk, caucasian, and appeared to be Australian and aged in their early 20s.

"There was a smell in the car and one of the guys sitting behind me did a poo," he said.

"The guys said 'don't stop the car'. I was scared. I stopped and jumped out of the car."

Mr Lalka said he called police but failed to get a response.

When the boys had gone and Mr Lalka returned to the car, he couldn't face the dump left in the footwell of the car.

"A guy was walking past and I just gave him $300 to clean the car," he said. "I don't know where he put it."

Mr Lalka, a driver for two years, said the $8 fare was unpaid. "I had a real bad headache because of the smell," he said.

"When I sleep, I feel the smell. I didn't have dinner last night.

"I talked to the base and they all started laughing. I don't want to do this any more. It's a s--- job.

"Some people say it's a s--- job. But actually, it is s---."

Taxi driver Kishan Lalka had a guy do a poo in the back of his taxi on Monday night. It put him off his dinner   Picture: ELISE DERWIN

ALL SET FOR BEER CAN REGATTA

STORY >> P5

BEST REAL ESTATE BARGAINS

>> P8,9 + MAGAZINE

FALL OF THE PALMO COUNCIL

>> SATURDAY EXTRA

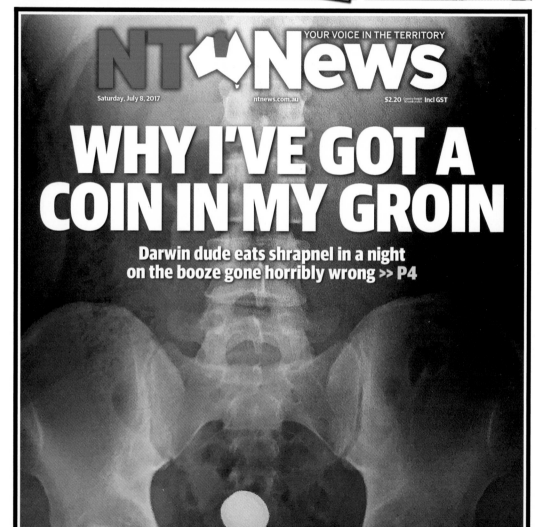

NT News

YOUR VOICE IN THE TERRITORY

Saturday, July 8, 2017 · ntnews.com.au · $2.20 Country bought $3 construction Incl GST

WHY I'VE GOT A COIN IN MY GROIN

Darwin dude eats shrapnel in a night on the booze gone horribly wrong >> P4

Always wear your seatbelt.

ENOUGH'S ENOUGH.

 NT POLICE, FIRE & EMERGENCY SERVICES

 M·ACC ROAD SAFETY · www.ntmacc.com.au

Stu's shrapnel wound

By Hayley Sorensen

A DARWIN professional has a lasting reminder to take it easy on the turps after he framed a 50c piece he swallowed during a night out and later excreted.

Stu, who didn't want to give his last name for fear of complete public humiliation and ruining his future employment prospects for the rest of his life, swallowed $2.70 in coins at Monsoons last Saturday night.

His memories of the Territory Day incident are fuzzy, but the 26-year-old said he woke on Sunday "feeling a bit crook".

"I went back to the bar and they said I should go to the hospital and the story slowly unravelled," he said.

Friends told Stu someone had dropped coins into a schooner he then skolled, currency included. An X-ray taken at Royal Darwin Hospital showed a 20c piece lodged near the base of his spine and a 50c piece in his oesophagus.

A $2 coin he is also believed to have swallowed had already made an exit. Stu said he managed to pass the 20c piece without noticing.

But the 50c coin proved more problematic. He underwent surgery to remove it from his oesophagus, but by the time surgeons opened him up, the coin had moved. It made its way out in a more organic way.

"I went fishing for turds; I had to get a pair of tongs out of my cousin's kitchen," Stu said.

"I guess I should get her new ones. Embarrassingly, I have to say it didn't hurt. I'm not too sure what that means, maybe something else happened to me that night."

The offending coin, minted in 1983, will be framed and kept in Stu's bedroom. The experience won't turn him off Monsoons.

"I might go back and sit in the pokies area with my mouth open," he said.

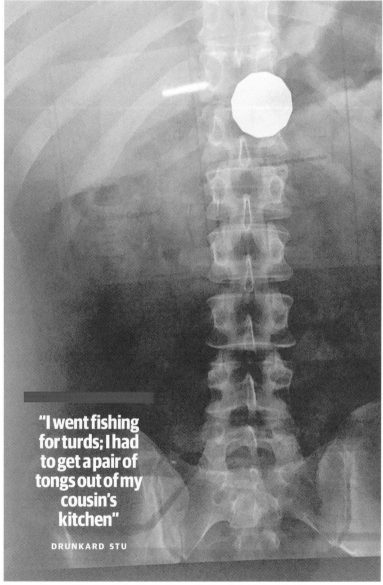

"I went fishing for turds; I had to get a pair of tongs out of my cousin's kitchen"

DRUNKARD STU

An x-ray shows a 50c piece lodged in Darwin professional Stu's internal system

NT News

YOUR VOICE IN THE TERRITORY

Tuesday, August 30, 2016 — ntnews.com.au — $1.40 Country freight 30 cents extra Incl GST

ULURU AS YOU'VE NEVER SEEN IT
PHOTO >> P7

MAKE THE MOST OF YOUR HARD-EARNED
MONEYSAVER HQ >> P23

How to play the fuel

GET YOUR 28-PAGE SUN NEWSPAPERS
POOL PUSH
>> INSIDE

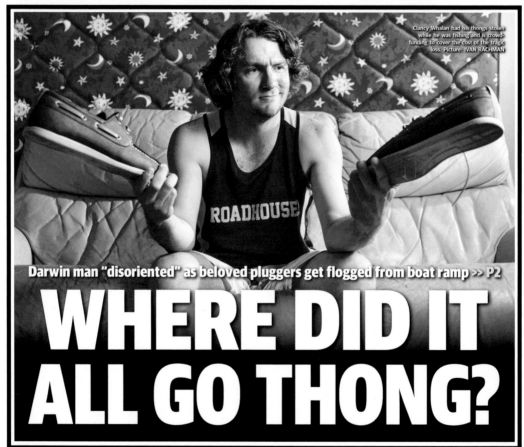

Clancy Whalan had his thongs stolen while he was fishing and is crowd-funding to cover the cost of the tragic loss. Picture: IVAN RACHMAN

ROADHOUSE

Darwin man "disoriented" as beloved pluggers get flogged from boat ramp >> P2

WHERE DID IT ALL GO THONG?

Labor's deputy in danger of losing

LABOR'S annointed Deputy Chief Minister Lynne Walker is in danger of losing her seat in Parliament.

In a huge shock, Ms Walker is trailing independent Yingiya Mark Guyula in the two-candidate preferred count 50.6 per cent to 49.4 per cent.

It is understood the party is deeply disappointed in possibly losing one of its strongest members.

While it has won the election with an overwhelming majority, Labor faces defeat in the seat of Blain with former Chief Minister-come independent Terry Mills leading high-profile candidate Damian Hale. Final results might not be known for another two weeks or longer because of absentee and postal ballots being accepted until September 9.

↘ **FULL STORY: P5**

Lynne Walker

Weather bureau keeps you in dark

STORMY weather, minimal tweets and a chance of unreturned calls are predicted over the next fortnight by the Bureau of Meteorology.

Australia-wide, Community and Public Sector Union (CPSU) members that work at the BoM will not be answering internal phone calls, updating Twitter or responding to the non-urgent media inquiries. CPSU deputy secretary Beth

Vincent-Pietsch said only union members would be taking industrial action over the next fortnight.

"The two weeks of smaller bans will put the BOM under pressure," she said.

Union members did not want to take industrial action but were "forced" to after an axe of allowances and three years without a pay raise.

↘ **FULL STORY: P7**

The BoM faces its own storm

Public asked to help foot the bill

By Lauren Roberts

DARWIN man Clancy Whalan is crowd-funding to replace his favourite pair of thongs after they were cruelly stolen from a boat ramp in Buffalo Creek.

Mr Whalan left his prized footwear on dry land early on Thursday morning to head out on a daylong fishing trip.

"My mate believes it's unlucky to bring them on the boat," Mr Whalan said.

"They're sentimental — they went everywhere with me." He said his "priceless" thongs were a Reef brand pair, with a bottle opener underneath, and a wealth of shared memories.

"You used to be able to leave your car unlocked — now you can't leave your thongs at a boat ramp," he said. "I'm just going barefoot now."

Mr Whalan said he was "forced" to wear a pair of enclosed shoes out over the weekend.

"I couldn't hack it," he confessed.

"I was out of place, it wasn't right ... I had to go home early." Housemate Brad Collins said Mr Whalan came home "shattered and upset" after his thongs were nicked last week.

"He was at a loss — disoriented," Mr Collins said.

"He's yet to recover and it's a week on." Mr Collins, a thong fan himself, said the tragic incident would make him think twice before leaving his pair behind on the beach.

Mr Whalan was hoping to raise $69 — enough to invest in some rather sturdy replacement footwear, but said nothing would replace the hole in his life the "priceless" thongs left behind. A NT Police spokeswoman said that thongs were a common piece of footwear in the Top End and that they were often removed and left unattended.

"I cannot recall any successful prosecutions with just stolen footwear — particularly thongs," she said.

"I would suggest there are not dedicated card-carrying thong thieves and that in most of these instances the theft is opportunistic."

Clancy Whalan had his thongs stolen while he was fishing over the weekend and is crowd-funding to cover the cost of the tragic loss　　Picture: IVAN RACHMAN

THE XXX FILES

TO risk stating the obvious, it's bloody hot in the Territory, especially in the Top End, so it makes sense that we like to get our clothes off. It's about embracing the pure and natural air conditioning, where the breeze flows freely against your skin. This attitude also makes us at ease with sex (or sexual references) on the front page. So, when the Aussie cricket team got caught cheating, our headline was a no-brainer and the winner, hands down. WHY I'VE GOT SOME STICKY NEAR MY DICKY reached millions of people on social media and put the world into a spin. Howzat!

YOUR CHANCE TO WIN BASSINTHEGRASS TICKETS
ENTERTAINMENT >> P13

FROM CROCS TO U.S COLLEGE BASKETBALL
>> SPORT

BOYS LAND THE 'BARRA SLAM' OF FISHING
ALEX JULIUS COLUMN >> P29

NT News

YOUR VOICE IN THE TERRITORY

Thursday, May 18, 2017   ntnews.com.au $1.40 Country Inside 50 cents extra Incl GST

Picture: JUSTIN KENNEDY

LET'S TALK ABOUT SEX

NEW SURVEY

Territory women the most satisfied in the nation — but 69 per cent want more spice in the bedroom >> P4

MAJOR UPGRADE COMING SOON

From May 26th 2017
Casuarina Square's Food Court
is undergoing refurbishment.

Indicative image only.

During works there will be
access changes for Prams,
Disabled and Trolleys for
approximately 6 weeks.

Visit casuarinasquare.com.au
for more details and
to determine your best
parking options.

Casuarina Square
by The GPT Group

NT News

YOUR VOICE IN THE TERRITORY

Wednesday, November 16, 2016

ntnews.com.au

$1.40 Country freight 30 cents extra Incl GST

ADELE'S DARWIN SNUB UPSETS LOYAL FANS

STORY >> P3

U.S. LOOKING AT TERRITORY FOR INVESTMENT

16-PAGE NT BUSINESS REVIEW >> INSIDE

COTCHIN, MITCHELL TO BE AWARDED 2012 BROWNLOW

>> SPORT

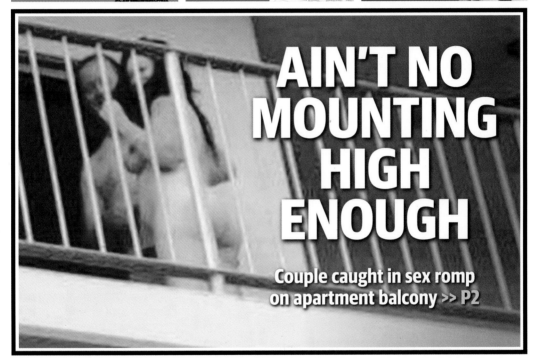

AIN'T NO MOUNTING HIGH ENOUGH

Couple caught in sex romp on apartment balcony >> P2

High-profile real estate agent investigated for missing money >> P4

CASH PROBE

Do you want to understand **property investment** & create a **property portfolio?**

NTPP is an independent investment property advisory company based in Darwin that has been successfully educating Territorians for over 10 years. We have a local team that will help you make the best decision on how and where to invest your money and time.

WE'LL TEACH YOU

- The basics of property investing.
- What makes a good real estate investment.
- How to structure a multi-property portfolio.
- How to finance & protect your investments.
- Use your tax to help pay for your property.
- Purchase with no money down.
- How to protect your principle home.
- The successful property investing principal of using capital growth to purchase more.

Keynote speaker and company founder, **Peter Spencer**, (featured in Mr Millionaire and Property Millionaire) will share a road map of proven principles and teach you how to build a multi-property portfolio.

LIMITED SEATS! ZERO FEES & CONTRACTS!

Speak with our panel of experts and learn how to reduce your tax and build real wealth through property investment!

Last workshop for 2016!
Thursday 24th November – 6pm for 6:15 start
Level 1,3 Nylander Street, Parap
RSVP Grant on 0432 199 771 or
via email grant@ntpropertypanel.com.au

BOOK YOUR FREE SEAT NOW!

Nude couple's balcony fun upsets neighbours

By Jill Poulsen

A COUPLE caught romping on the balcony of their Stuart Park apartment was "unperturbed" to learn their nudity was on full display to neighbours.

A man who also lives in the complex took a picture on Saturday afternoon to document the act he described as "offensive".

When the onlooker told the woman that there were kids playing in the adjacent park who might be able to see the nude couple, she simply "twerked" at him. "When it's in complete public view, I see it as (no different from) standing on your front lawn," he said.

"She was completely unperturbed … the guy ran inside though and put some skin coloured underwear on."

"She didn't go inside until I told her I would be contacting body corporate about it."

The neighbour said the nude display was part of ongoing "disruptive" behaviour by the tenant.

"Quite frankly I'm sick of the treatment," he said. "I'm not sure who the bloke was with her, but he definitely was not her husband."

The man said he didn't believe the pair was having sex at the time he spied them.

"They were just giggling and smoking cigarettes," he said.

An NT Police spokeswoman said a couple flashing their uglies could be found guilty of offensive conduct. The penalty is $2000, up to six months in prison, or both.

The nude couple isn't the first to draw a crowd while baring their bits. In 2011, a Darwin couple made national news after getting it on in broad daylight in the La Grande apartments on the corner of Mitchell and Knuckey streets.

In 2010, a survey of more than 10,000 men and women revealed that almost every second Territorian enjoyed having sex in public — from beaches to bathrooms, offices to nightclubs.

It seems little has changed in the past six years.

> ## "I'm not sure who the bloke was ... but he definitely was not her husband."
>
> **NEIGHBOUR**

Nude people on a balcony in Stuart Park   Picture: SUPPLIED

NT News

YOUR VOICE IN THE TERRITORY

Tuesday, November 15, 2016   ntnews.com.au $1.40 Country freight 20 cents extra Incl GST

OUR SUPER MOON WAS AWESOME

... How was yours? >> P2

Picture: JUSTIN KENNEDY

Defence base emergency as naked man runs amok >> P2

NUDE RUDE DUDE FORCES LOCKDOWN

FAST FACT #1

1 in 5 of all deaths and serious injuries on Territory roads involves speeding.

Speeding is the fastest way to lose control.

MACC
ROAD SAFETY

www.ntmacc.com.au

Rare moon super sight for lunar lovers

By Lauren Roberts

ONE moon capturing universal attention of late is the rare super moon. According to NASA, last night's lunar event was the closest the full moon had been to the Earth since 1948.

But, don't worry if you missed it, Darwin astronomer Geoff Carr said tonight's moon could be even better. Mr Carr said last night's moon rose before the sunset but tonight's would rise while the sky was dark. He said the moon would only be "marginally" further away this evening.

"People like rare things ... there's been a huge amount of interest (in the super moon)," he said.

"People have a love affair with the moon, they write songs about the moon. "

Mr Carr said Darwin had no hills so the super moon could be viewed from most of the city, and was scheduled to rise about 8pm.

Lucky Territorians were treated to another rare sight this morning, as one arse bared all for *NT News* front page notoriety. The popular term 'mooning' arose from the similarities between a bare bottom and the moon's smooth, white surface.

The super moon pokes through the thick cloud from a Darwin storm at Stokes Hill Wharf. Last night's event was the closest the full moon has been to Earth since 1948
Picture: ELISE DERWIN

Nude intruder sparks Defence base drama

By Hayley Sorensen

A NUDE intruder who triggered a lockdown at Defence Establishment Berrimah is on the loose.

A Defence spokeswoman confirmed the base went into lockdown when an intruder was found on site Wednesday. Police were called to apprehend the man but he scaled a fence and fled before they arrived.

The *NT News* understands the man approached a Defence member and two removalists on site — with his weapon on display — and spent some time wandering around base.

The unclothed interloper was reportedly approached by a private security contractor who kept him occupied by giving him forms to fill out.

It's believed the man was spooked by the arrival of another security guard at the base, leading him to climb a fence. He reportedly entered a security vehicle before fleeing on foot. The Defence spokeswoman said the unadorned invader was no threat to the safety of anyone on base at the time. "Defence Establishment Berrimah was in lock down for a brief period and during this time there was no danger to any defence personnel or contractors," she said.

Defence did not respond to questions from the *NT News* as to whether the incident would spark a security protocol review at the Berrimah base, or provide any details to explain how he was able to enter the fenced compound which is protected by 24-hour security guards.

CHAMPION JOCK BOWS OUT AFTER 49 YEARS

INSPIRING >> P3

HUMPTY DOO DAD SETS FIRE TO SON'S DOPE PLANTS

STORY >> P7

CELEBRATING A BRILLIANT TWO DECADES OF MUSIC NT

ENTERTAINMENT>> P15

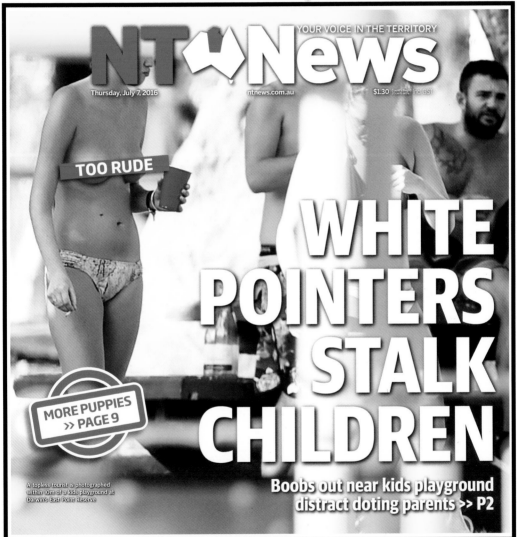

NT News

YOUR VOICE IN THE TERRITORY

Thursday, July 7, 2016 · ntnews.com.au · $1.30 Country $1.60 (incl GST)

TOO RUDE

MORE PUPPIES >> PAGE 9

WHITE POINTERS STALK CHILDREN

Boobs out near kids playground distract doting parents >> P2

A topless tourist is photographed within 10m of a kids playground at Darwin's East Point Reserve

RE-FRESH YOUR FUN AT

NOW OPEN

The **Quarter**

OPEN DAILY 9AM – LATE

RESTAURANTS
KIDS PLAY
ENTERTAINMENT
CINEMA
FITNESS

f ⊙ casuarinasquare.com.au

Casuarina Square
by The GPT Group

GPT Property Management Pty Limited trading as part of The GPT Group

White pointers stalk children at playground

By Judith Aisthorpe

SCHOOL'S out and so are backpacker boobs.

As kids enjoyed the school break so too did this bunch of young backpackers at East Point — right next to a playground.

While the children were playing seemingly unaware that only 10m away women were topless, several parents did notice — including at least one observant father.

At least three topless women in a group of around 30 were last week spotted lazing about watching friends play volleyball while others cooked up a barbecue as music played in the background. Almost all the partygoers were dressed in swimwear.

If you do get the urge to strip down, take note there are only two public spaces in Darwin where you can legally bare you buns — the Darwin Waterfront, where women can sunbake and swim topless, and a designated nude area at Casuarina Beach.

Darwin Waterfront Corporation said nude and female topless sunbaking was not allowed at the Wave Lagoon. However, female topless sunbaking and swimming was allowed at the Recreation Lagoon.

If caught by police in an undesignated nudist area you could be stung with a hefty fine of $432 and charged with offensive behaviour.

Millner resident Amanda O'Keefe brought her two sons down to East Point to play at the playground with visiting family friends and their kids and said she wasn't fussed about there being topless women.

She said she usually heads down to the park but this was the first time women had been topless while she was there.

"It certainly didn't surprise me," she said.

"It's a distraction for the parents who are trying to watch their kids."

Ms O'Keefe said she was waiting for her kids to realise but suspected they hadn't noticed because they weren't aware of social norms. Ewan Wright was down at the park with his wife and two kids and said while it wasn't offensive they could have moved a bit further away from the playground.

"It's not appropriate, they could have taken it away from the kids a bit further," he said.

His wife, however, wasn't fussed.

People looking to get nude in a more private setting can head out to a number of locally owned nudist camping locations in the rural area.

Women walk around with their boobs out on display while partying with friends next to a children's playground at East Point Reserve

66

CRICKET'S DARKEST DAY

Monday, March 26, 2018   ntnews.com.au $1.60 Country freight 30 cents extra Incl GST

YOUR VOICE IN THE TERRITORY

NT News

We're for *you*

Player Cameron Bancroft after placing stickytape into his trousers during a Test match in South Africa

Picture: ASHLEY VLOTMAN

WHY I'VE GOT SOME STICKY NEAR MY DICKY

Heads expected to roll after Aussie team caught cheating red-handed

REPORTS P4-5, BOLT, WICKING, SPORT

Damning report into Batchelor

SCOOP

ALLEGATIONS of financial neglect and questionable recruitment methods are at the centre of a damning report into education provider Batchelor Institute, the *NT News* can reveal. The probe has discovered the organisation had more than $15 million of operational losses from 2014 to 2017 and a budget blowout of $2.151 million in 2016.

The Assurance Advisory Group's report reveals a litany of "severe risks" that are threatening the organisation's existence.

This comes as a new chief executive starts at the organisation today.

↘ **REPORTS P7**

Rubbish man a council chance

SHOCK

A MAN who has stripped naked in Darwin courtrooms multiple times is within 80 votes of an alderman position on Palmerston Council.

The so-called Rubbish Warrior, Trevor Jenkins, is one of three candidates all capable of catching sacked former mayor Ian Abbott who currently holds the seventh and final position with 559 primary votes.

A recount and the distribution of preferences is set to occur this week.

Former jailbird and Palmerston mayor Rob Macleod is still a strong chance to take back the reins of the satellite city.

↘ **FULL STORY P8**

The story behind *that* cricket headline

THE *NT News'* "Why I've Got Some Sticky Near My Dicky" headline which has the world talking was devised at a kids' play cafe in suburban Darwin.

NT News editor Matt Williams and deputy editor Ken McGregor's three-year-old children were playing at Planet Tenpin in Nightcliff on Sunday afternoon when possible headlines were being bandied around by the *NT News* editorial bosses.

Williams said to McGregor the Australian cricket ball tampering scandal was one of the biggest stories of the year and the *NT News* had an obligation to deliver a cracking headline.

Matt Garrick, who was editing from the office, sent the first version of the front page which carried the headline "Balls On The Line". Williams and McGregor agreed it was a great headline but started racking their brains for something which could captivate the nation.

"We've got a reputation to uphold, mate, there's got to be something that can stand out from the crowd," Williams said to McGregor.

After a few failed attempts at bettering the "Balls On The Line" headline, it was McGregor who eventually came up with the genius of "Why I've Got Some Sticky Near My Dicky."

McGregor, who played 152 AFL games for the Adelaide Crows between 1999 and 2008 before moving into journalism, said the headline was perfect for the *NT News* brand.

"We've had some cracking headlines with a similar rhyme over the years, including two of our most famous ones — 'Why I've Got A Cracker Up My Clacker' and 'Why I've Got A Packer Up My Clacker'," he said.

"I just started thinking about headlines starting with 'Why I've Got' and it just eventuated from there."

Williams said the cricket scandal headline was on track to be the most viewed on social media in Australian history.

"We had a same-sex marriage front page last year which reached more than 2 million people on social media, making it the most viewed front page in Australia ever, but we think this one's going to top it," he said. At 10.30am on Monday, the cricket scandal front page had been viewed 561,000 times on Twitter and had reached 755,000 people on Facebook.

"Kenny played in front of some big crowds when he played for the Crows but he hasn't played in front of a bigger crowd with this headline!" Williams said.

"Kenny didn't get many Brownlow votes during his AFL career but for this headline I'm giving him the three, the two and the one. Just brilliant!"

Former Adelaide Crows player turned *NT News* deputy editor, Ken McGregor.

SUNDAY Territorian

June 26, 2016 $1.40 Country freight 20c extra. Includes GST

WOMEN, THE NORTH NEEDS YOU...

Yoanna Williams and her fellow women are outnumbered by men in the Top End. Statistics show the Territory is the most male-dominated part of Australia
Picture: IVAN RACHMAN

BEAUTY CALL

Experts say our sheila shortage is holding the Territory back
Why it's a bigger problem than you think >> P4

FREE GLOSSY FASHION MAG TOKEN >> P8

TERRITORY FOOD AND FASHION >> **FRONTIER**

AWESOME SCHOOL HOLIDAY FUN >> P3,6

MASSIVE $38,500 BINGO JACKPOT >> P61

FUNKY MONKS 3PM TODAY @ HOWARD SPRINGS TAV!

The NT's a sausagefest

... and that's a bigger problem than you think

By Judith Aisthorpe

THE Northern Territory's sheila shortage is showing no signs of abating.

The latest population figures from the Australian Bureau of Statistics show there's 112 Territory blokes for every 100 ladies, the highest male to female ratio in Australia.

WA is the only other state that has a ratio where there are more males than females at 102 to 100.

In a sliver of good news for hard-up fellas, at least the sausage fest has remained stable — the NT ratio is unchanged from last year.

The abundance of men can be put down to strong demand in the construction and defence industries.

But the statistics don't indicate how many eligible bachelors there are. They also don't take into account the presence of Mitchell Street's conquering force, the US Marines.

Central Australian-based South African Patrick Hannigan agreed finding a woman in the Territory was tough, even for a single bloke in his prime. "It is a jungle out there. Sometimes it is like trying to find a needle in a haystack," he said.

The dateless desperado listed the Rock Bar in Alice Springs as his "hunting ground" and said he didn't have the luxury of being picky.

Law student Yoanna Williams, 22, said while the odds were good, the goods were often odd.

She said the discrepancy was most evident on the Monsoons' dance floor.

But she reckoned Territory men lost their nerve without liquid courage.

"No one's going to come up to you in the supermarket and talk to you," she said.

Ms Williams said she was struggling to find a man with brains in a sea of beer swilling, odd-smelling blockheads.

She remained hopeful though and said post-codes had nothing to do with finding the right person.

She had one suggestion for men looking to cut through the clutter.

"Be nice and say hello and maybe make a joke; I like to laugh," she said.

Wanted: More women

Yoanna Williams says while the odds of finding a bloke in Darwin are good (20:1) ... often the goods are odd

Picture: IVAN RACHMAN

Tuesday, February 14, 2017   ntnews.com.au $1.40 Casual Retail incl GST

NT News

YOUR VOICE IN THE TERRITORY

A weird-looking passionfruit has been growing in the backyard of a Darwin home
Picture: IVAN RACHMAN

FRUIT OF THE GROINS

Get your mind out of the gutter ... it's just a passionfruit growing in a Darwin backyard STORY >> P2

DANNY — CHAMPION OF THE WORLD **ROALD DAHL BOOK ONLY $2.60**
TOKEN >> P3

'UNDERBELLY' STYLE EXECUTION IN THE DESERT: COURT HEARS
EXCLUSIVE >> P4

Phallic fruit a true NT miracle

By Judith Aisthorpe

A SEEDY passionfruit vine has produced not one — but two — phallic shaped fruits.

The yellow passionfruit vine belongs to Bakewell resident Jane Hewitt.

It was planted around two years ago but only started producing fruit at the end of last year.

The penis-shaped fruit — which the *NT News* is proud to reveal on Valentine's Day — came as a surprise to Ms Hewitt and her husband.

It doesn't seem like it's an odd freak of nature either after she found a second fruit bearing an uncanny resemblance.

She said they were waiting for a third fruit to grow a bit more to see if it would follow suit. "I bought it as a yellow passionfruit vine from Bunnings, it's been so funny," she said. The two penis-shaped fruits have been growing since Christmas and are now quite large.

"[It's] probably about 9 inches long and very fat," she said. The grandmother said that she hadn't pointed out the fruits to her grandkids so as to avoid having to explain their peculiar shape. While the plant is lush and healthy, Ms Hewitt admitted that she didn't know how to tell if a passionfruit was ripe or not.

Darwin woman Jane Hewitt has been growing a penis shaped passionfruit which is nine inches long

Wednesday, December 6, 2017

ntnews.com.au

$1.60 Country freight 30 cents extra Incl GST

YOUR VOICE IN THE TERRITORY
News

This couple enjoyed the Top End sun that Darwin has on offer at a CBD apartment building – and provided an eyeful for the locals

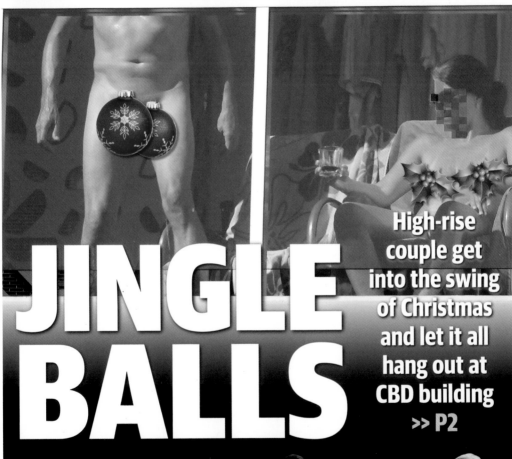

JINGLE BALLS

High-rise couple get into the swing of Christmas and let it all hang out at CBD building
>> P2

TERRITORY'S GREEN ANT GIN GOES WILD
>> NT BUSINESS REVIEW

PARRA EELS SLIP INTO THE RED CENTRE
STORY >> P3

120 MOST POWERFUL: 80-61
Today exclusively on
news.com.au

Daring Darwin pair just grin and bare it

By Hayley Sorensen

WHEN the Top End heats up, sometimes there's nothing to do but strip down.

That's what this Darwin couple chose to do on the balcony of their CBD apartment.

The emancipated exhibitionists shed their clothes to enjoy the Territory sunshine in their uglies at the Zen building in Carey St. It was unclear if their choice of attire was to celebrate the onset of the festive season but, as these pictures show, there were plenty of white boomers and jingle bells on display.

One witness, who didn't want to be named for fear of being publicly branded a pervert, said she had the Christmas classic stuck in her head all day.

"At first I thought they were wearing nude swimsuits but upon closer inspection I saw, in great detail, their private parts dangling about," she said.

"I probably looked longer than was kosher but it was an absolutely mesmerising sight."

With a fortnight of shirts hung behind them to dry, the pair weren't short of clothing options, but elected to get about in the raw instead. In a concession to safety, they slung towels over their chairs to minimise the risk of sustaining burns to their delicate regions.

As they evened out their tan lines, the woman sipped on a dark coloured drink as her companion enjoyed a durry.

A bottle of what appeared to be sunscreen sat on a table behind the pair.

Both seemed unfazed by the prospect of being spotted by neighbours or passers-by, as the male half of the couple stood up to flash his plums.

Territorians have a long and proud history of flaunting their nads from high-rise buildings. Last year, neighbours of a Stuart Park couple copped an eyeful as residents romped in their birthday suits on an apartment balcony. When told they might be spotted by children, the woman performed a defiant twerk. In 2011, a Darwin couple got down to business on the balcony of the La Grande apartments on the corner of Mitchell and Knuckey streets.

A couple was seen enjoying the Darwin sun in the nuddy

GROW YOUR OWN CHIVES
$2.50 WITH COUPON >> P2

GRANNY SNARED IN COP STING
STORY >> P5

NORTHERN TERRITORY POLICE
TO SERVE and PROTECT

THE LATEST IN TERRITORY BUSINESS NEWS
NTBR STARTS >> P13

NT Business
REVIEW
Australian industry encouraged to the NT

Wednesday, September 5, 2018   ntnews.com.au $1.70 Country freight 10 cents extra **Incl GST**

We're for *you*

NT NEWS

YOUR VOICE IN THE TERRITORY

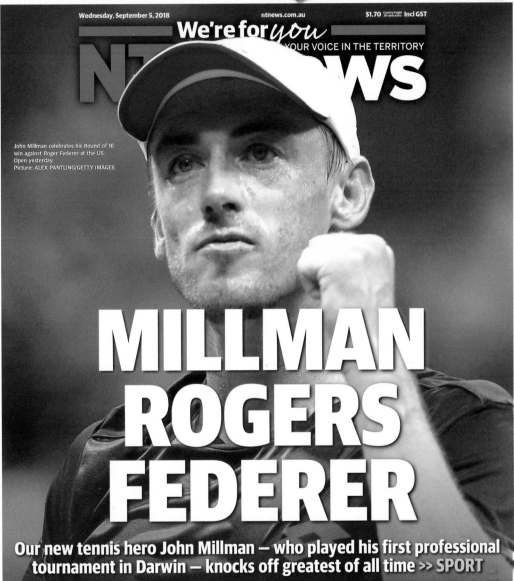

John Millman celebrates his Round of 16 win against Roger Federer at the US Open yesterday
Picture: ALEX PANTLING/GETTY IMAGES

MILLMAN ROGERS FEDERER

Our new tennis hero John Millman — who played his first professional tournament in Darwin — knocks off greatest of all time >> SPORT

SHOCK We're drinking less booze: ABS

AUSSIES are passing up beer and drinking the least amount of alcohol in 50 years.

New data released by the Australian Bureau of Statistics shows 186 million litres of alcohol was consumed by Australians in 2016-17, the lowest levels seen since the 1960s.

ABS director of health stat-

istics Louise Gates said a drop in beer consumption had been driving the trend, with an average decline of 2.4 per cent per year over the last 10 years.

Darwin beer enthusiast Stewart 'Stretch' McAvoy said most Territorians loved their beer and believed the decline represents more of what was

happening in the states down south. "A lot of Territorians still drink beer, they definitely drink more than other states because of the hotter climate up here," he said.

"Getting a beer to cool off and unwind … is like second nature."

↘ **P3: FULL STORY**

Aircon warnings ignored: emails

A CHEAPER fire-resistant alternative to the fibreglass air-conditioning insulation used on the new $206 million Palmerston Regional Hospital was presented as an option to Government.

The *NT News* has obtained emails to the Department of Infrastructure, Planning and

Logistics outlining the approved product and expressing frustration at the locally available product being ignored.

"I am sure we had multiple meetings (2016-17), face-to-face, along with countless emails of info and spec data, actually chains of emails (more than happy to share these

emails with you to jog your memories?), regarding the dangers of fibreglass and offering you a lower costing alternative … people in your departments, along with you, need to be held accountable for actions of signing off on these preventable outcomes."

↘ **P11: FULL STORY**

CLOSE ENCOUNTERS OF THE NT KIND

ALIENS and UFOs are intrinsically linked to the Territory. Do they really exist? Is the truth out there? We think it is.

When eight ducks disappeared from a rural property with no sign of forced entry or leftovers, it could only mean one thing, right?

They were without any shadow of a doubt ABDUCKTED.

And when a heap of mangoes simply disappeared from a backyard tree you know exactly what happened ... there could be no other explanation. Well, at least as far as an *NT News* journalist is concerned.

GREAT WEEKEND READING

INSIDE NTWeekend TODAY

WHATS NEXT FOR CYRIL RIOLI

HOW TO STOP KIDS' TANTRUMS

14 PAGES OF SPORT PLUS 8-PAGE FORM GUIDE

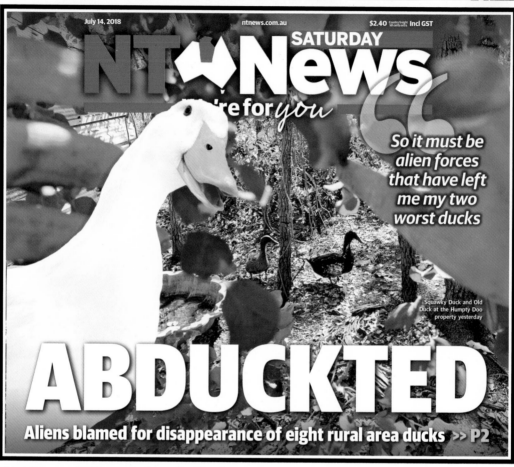

July 14, 2018 ntnews.com.au $2.40 Country freight 60 cents extra Incl GST

SATURDAY NT News

We're for *you*

So it must be alien forces that have left me my two worst ducks

Squawky Duck and Old Duck at the Humpty Doo property yesterday

ABDUCKTED

Aliens blamed for disappearance of eight rural area ducks >> P2

Territory AFL matches in limbo

EXCLUSIVE

THE future of AFL matches in the Territory is in limbo as Melbourne Football Club's current deal with the NT Government ends this year.

The league is looking at all possibilities for future hosts but AFL media manager Patrick Keane said this year's games had been a success.

He said there was no decision yet as to who would play future Territory games from 2019 and beyond. "We were very pleased with both games, with Alice Springs and in last week's game at TIO stadium," he said. "We've had an initial discussion about our presence in the Territory this year, there will be some more discussions soon, we have an intention to play next year ... we're still in the process at the moment.

"From AFL point of view, we obviously want to have a presence in the NT ... "
↘ **P5: FULL STORY**

Donghai set to increase Darwin flights

EXCLUSIVE

TOURISM Minister Lauren Moss says only final regulatory approval stands between China's Donghai Airlines increasing its direct flight service from Shenzhen to Darwin to three times a week.

Ms Moss confirmed reports that the airline is working toward introducing a third weekly rotation for the month of August operating on Fridays.

"This is great news and reinforces Donghai's commitment to making the route successful, bringing new Chinese tourists to Darwin," she said. "The Northern Territory Government understands that Donghai Airlines is awaiting final regulatory approval and August 3 is the planned start date. This is a strong vote of confidence in the Territory.

"Since the inaugural flight ... more Chinese travellers have become aware of the route."
↘ **P9: FULL STORY**

SKYCITY DARWIN

Sunsets AND GOOD VIBES

$15,000 IN CASH PRIZES TO BE WON TONIGHT!
1 x $5,000 & 1 x $10,000

IT'S FREE TO ENTER!

7 July - 26 August 2018. Terms and conditions apply. Permit number TLP1022. Please gamble responsibly

Collect your wristband on arrival from 6pm.

'I'm not quackers but aliens stole my ducks'

By Lauren Roberts

"ALIEN forces" are behind a series of strange duckling disappearances in Humpty Doo, fears NT nurse Desi Friend.

About two months ago, one of Ms Friend's ducks went missing – then another, and a third – until a total of eight ducks went missing from her locked yard.

"Mysteriously over the course of two weeks, one by one they disappeared into thin air," she said.

"There's no sign of any forced entry, there's no feathers, there's no big fat snakes, there's no dogs, there's no evidence at all.

"A wild dog couldn't have got past my dog and would have left feathers or a mess – and a snake couldn't have eaten eight ducks in three weeks."

The birds had clipped wings and couldn't fly, so Ms Friend said it was unlikely her feathered friends escaped themselves. However, she hadn't ruled out the possibility of an alien abduction.

"That's definitely on the cards," she said. "Whoever has taken the ducks has taken all the good ducks, and I've been left with Squawky Duck and Old Duck, who is a bit senile.

"So it must be alien forces that have left me my two worst ducks."

Ms Friend has chickens, horses and a rooster in the same enclosure – all of whom escaped the aliens' grasp.

It's the first time pets have been pinched from the Humpty Doo animal lover, which she said must be an indication of their fine taste. "They must prefer ducks," Ms Friend said.

"They were Muscovy ducks so they were massive – at least double the size of the regular ones."

Looking around her 4.5ha property, Ms Friend said there were worse places for an alien to touch down. "There's space to land the spaceship," she said.

The abducktion ranks four out of five Gerrys on the Gerrymeter, the metric used by the *NT News* to gauge the credibility of extraterrestrial-related news. The Gerrymeter is named in honour of Nelson MLA Gerry Wood, the NT's most trustworthy politician and occasional UFO spotter.

It's not the first time something strange has been reported in Darwin's rural area.

Earlier this year, McMinns Lagoon amateur astronomer Peter Tibbits reported an object soaring through the night sky. "It was like a drop of white paint on a black bit of cardboard," he said.

Late last year, Batchelor resident Sue Fitzgerald said three UFOs covered in red lights came soaring over her home.

The three bright circles were moving towards a floating white orb, she said. "It was travelling so effortlessly."

Squawky Duck is one of two ducks that remain on a Humpty Doo property after 'aliens struck'

SACKED FROM THE AIRWAVES
TERRITORY FM SCANDAL >> P4

AUSSIES ON VERGE OF FIRST TEST GLORY
>> SPORT

HO, HO, HOT! SEA OF SANTAS FLOOD DARWIN
PICS AND STORY >> P8-9

NT News

YOUR VOICE IN THE TERRITORY

Monday, November 27, 2017   ntnews.com.au $1.60 Country Freight 10 cents extra Incl GST

TENNANT FREAK

UFO captured hovering above outback street on Google Maps >> P2

A flying saucer captured hovering above Ambrose St in Tennant Creek
Picture: GOOGLE STREET VIEW

AND Territorians still smoking most pot in the nation >> P3

Darwin detour ends in flight-mare

A FLIGHT to Bali turned into a 25-hour nightmare for passengers after it was forced to touch down in Darwin when Mt Agung erupted.

Flight JQ37 left Sydney on Saturday evening for a six-hour flight, but was forced to turn around short of Denpasar Airport because of ash spewing from the volcano.

The Jetstar plane's 320 passengers were taken to Darwin, then flown to Cairns because the Northern Territory capital had no accommodation.

While in Darwin, four men en route for Schoolies were removed from the plane by the Australian Federal Police because of their rowdiness. It's understood the men have gone on to fly to Bali.

↘ Reports: P6

Two hurt in remote rollover

TWO young men have been plucked to safety by a Care-Flight chopper after being seriously injured in a rollover on a remote Territory highway.

A 16-year-old and a 22-year-old were flown to Royal Darwin Hospital with suspected spinal injuries on Saturday afternoon after their car flipped on a stretch of road between Oenpelli and Maningrida.

A Health Department spokeswoman confirmed both men were still in stable conditions yesterday. The incident came just a day after an 80-year-old woman had to be flown from the Bynoe region with head injuries and a laceration to her left arm, sustained in another road crash.

↘ Photos and story: P5

Alien encounter on the road to Tennant Creek

By Judith Aisthorpe

DARWIN resident Dean Stocks reckons this is the weirdest thing he's seen sober.

He could not believe his eyes when he saw a potential UFO pop up on his computer screen while using Google Maps to search for an address in Tennant Creek.

Clicking on the Ambrose St location, and zooming in with Google Street View, his jaw nearly hit the ground. Hovering above the outback town is an object posing a remarkable similarity to a flying saucer. He said he hadn't decided if it was a sky boob or a bona fide UFO, but knew it was out of the ordinary.

"I don't believe I've seen a sky boob before but I've read about them in picture magazines," he said.

"I know all the conspirators will have their say – it will be a reflection of the Tennant Creek watertank or something like that."

He said it was one of the most phenomenal things he'd ever seen, even behind the computer in Darwin. Mr Stocks said he travelled to Tennant Creek every few weeks and would be driving down Ambrose St to see if there was anything paranormal floating above the surface next time he was down there.

Darwin astronomer Geoff Carr said the image was likely photoshopped.

International alien group, Mutual UFO Network have developed a comprehensive database of UFO sightings around the world. The UFO Stalker map includes dates, times and details of the incident.

One Palmerston resident described a fireball-like object in the sky which hovered above her and then changed direction in June 2007. It gave off dull crackling noises and heat, her report stated.

A report in September 2015 detailed an incident in January 2014 by a storm chaser who described seeing two flying objects flying near a storm cell.

To check out reported UFO sightings head to mufon.com.

The highway to Tennant Creek is known as a hotspot for UFOs

NT  News

YOUR VOICE IN THE TERRITORY

Wednesday, December 7, 2016   ntnews.com.au   **$1.40** Country freight 30 cents extra **Incl GST**

MUSIC FESTIVAL IN STICKY SITUATION
STORY >> P3

TERRITORY ZEROES IN ON DEFENCE OPPORTUNITIES
NT BUSINESS REVIEW >> INSIDE

NT Business REVIEW
INSIDE
Billions of defence dollars up for grabs
THE WEEK AHEAD

DID ALIENS STEAL MY MANGOES?

Palmo resident shocked as hundreds of mangoes vanish from backyard tree >> P2

Warren Fisher had all but one mango stolen from his backyard tree
Picture: ELISE DERWIN

EXCLUSIVE: Commission facing years of delays and cost blowouts >> P6

ROYAL SHAMBLES

NORTH CREST

COMING SOON
NEW LAND RELEASE

LIFESTYLE   LIVING   LEISURE   northcrest.com.au

Mangoes mystery as back-yard tree stripped overnight

By Judith Aisthorpe

IT'S enough to give anyone a serious case of mango madness.

The Fishers of Moulden were left dumbfounded on Saturday morning when they stepped outside to see their mango tree stripped of hundreds of mangoes.

Only one juicy fruit was left hanging on the tree and not a single half-eaten one on the ground.

Either there's an expert mango thief on the loose or aliens were responsible, as the Palmerston residents were unable to explain how the tree in their backyard was ransacked.

Warren Fisher said friends were visiting on Saturday to pick some of the fruit.

"I can't explain it. I just know that we had hundreds on Friday and the next day there was just one," he said.

"There were no mangoes on the ground."

His mother, Rita Fisher, reckoned humans couldn't have been responsible.

"It's not human because the tree's too big to get up there. It's a mystery," she said. "There wasn't even a chewed mango on the ground."

Further adding to the mystery, Ms Fisher's two dogs didn't bark on the night.

Warren Fisher had all but one mango stolen from his tree in his backyard in Moulden

Picture: ELISE DERWIN

NT News

YOUR VOICE IN THE TERRITORY

Thursday, October 13, 2016 — ntnews.com.au — $1.40 Country freight 30 cents extra Incl GST

CLASSIFIED

AIR FORCE SURRENDERS NT AIRSPACE TO UFO INVADERS

READ THE SECRET REPORT >> P2

october BUSINESS month 2016

Register now for a range of inspirational and educational business events

SCOTT BOOCOCK
YES TO INNOVATION
Darwin
28 October
6.30pm - 10pm
Darwin Convention Centre

TODD SAMPSON
POWER OF CREATIVITY
Darwin
31 October
6.30am - 9am
Darwin Convention Centre

f in
obm.nt.gov.au

PLATINUM SPONSORS

nab
CHARLES DARWIN UNIVERSITY

MEDIA SPONSORS

mix

Sun969
8HA
fm 104.1
9

Imparja

NORTHERN TERRITORY GOVERNMENT

Open to UFO invasion

By Jill Poulsen

IN a blow for Territorians, the Royal Australian Air Force doesn't care if you've seen an unidentified flying object.

Where once the RAAF would investigate reports of UFOs — which it calls unusual aerial sightings — it now refers them to specialist UFO watchers.

Newly surfaced documents previously marked secret, obtained by Fairfax Media, revealed the RAAF stopped looking into UFO reports in the 1990s because only about three per cent of sightings could not be explained. Most sightings were found to be attributable to aircraft, satellites, meteors, space debris, stars and planets. The Department of Defence didn't announce the change at the time, fearing conspiracy theories.

President of UFO Research Queensland Sheryl Gottschall described the change as "deeply disturbing".

"It's a bit of a slap in the face for groups to be expected to be doing that, I would say it's deeply disturbing that they are not investigating those reports," she said.

"I think that they do take it seriously, it's just that for public record that's what they're saying."

In 1994, all UFO civilian groups received a letter from the Department of Defence saying the RAAF wasn't taking reports from the public because they felt the public was better serviced by civilian groups, Ms Gottschall said.

The letter, obtained by the *NT News*, stated: "In future, the RAAF will not accept reports of UAS and will not attempt to assign cause or comment on the reliability of particular sightings".

Ms Gottschall said: "I thought that was a bit of a joke considering we're all volunteers." She said she had spoken to many people since then who had called the RAAF base at Amberley, west of Brisbane, to report a suspect flying object but were not taken seriously.

The number of sightings reported to the organisation fluctuated, Ms Gottschall said.

"People report their sightings differently now, they report through social media, they report it to international locations via the internet and quite possibly there's been a change in the phenomenon as well," she said.

When approached for comment, Chief Minister Michael Gunner would not be drawn on whether the government was keeping its eyes on the Territory's skies.

"The Government can neither confirm nor deny the existence of a specialist NT UFO Investigative Unit," he said.

Uncovered documents reveal the NT could be susceptible to UFOs

KILLER'S MIDNIGHT ARREST

EXCLUSIVE >> P5

DANIEL LUTHUR HEISS 290565 890623

DEMONS SEAL DEAL AND EASY WIN

>> SPORT

8-PAGE CARNIVAL LIFTOUT

>> INSIDE

SUNDAY Territorian

July 10, 2016

$1.40 Country freight 20c extra. Includes GST

STRANGERS IN OUR SKIES

Humpty Doo gardener left baffled after forces from above kill trees

JILL POULSEN REPORTS
>> P4

Are UFOs killing Mike Mewett's trees in Humpty Doo?

Picture: ELISE DERWIN

That's why I pick Woolies

woolworths.com.au/pickwoolies

Woolworths
The fresh food people

UFO drops load on Doo

By Jill Poulsen

A BAFFLING case of dying foliage has a Humpty Doo man questioning what's been lurking in the skies over his 2ha rural property.

It was just under a week ago when Mike Mewett first noticed patches of leaves on trees on a roughly 100m section of the property were dropping.

"It's so strange, it's not the tree that's dying, it's like there's something been dropped on it from above," he said.

"To me that's the only logical explanation, unless we've got aliens around here."

The *NT News* visited Mr Mewett's property and witnessed the triangular-shaped section of trees where parts of a tree's branch had completely died while other leaves on the branch flourished.

Mr Mewett, an avid gardener, said he'd never encountered anything like it.

"We sometimes see a light aircraft flying in the area ... maybe it dumped some fuel," he said.

Mr Mewett's Humpty Doo property is less than a kilometre from where Brisbane UFO hunter Erik Black spotted a "thing" floating above his head in 2010. Mr Black described the UFO as "shaped like a hamburger, with black dots" and "weird-looking headlights".

Several recent sightings of similar, round orbs hovering silently above Humpty Doo have also been reported to the *NT News*.

A local arborist said that without inspecting the damage on Mr Mewett's property, it was hard to say what the cause was, but said it definitely didn't sound like a virus.

"Sometimes lightning strikes can cause damage like that but if it spans 100m it wouldn't be a lightning strike, plus we haven't had any lightning," he said.

"It could be a reaction to a chemical ... it certainly does sound strange."

The rural area is also known for its Yowie activity, but a local Yowie expert, who asked not to be named, said there was "no way" the damage on Mr Mewett's property could be put down to those creatures.

"It's far more likely to be a UFO than a Yowie," he said.

"It's so strange, it's not the tree that's dying, it's like there's something been dropped on it from above"

Has a UFO dropped its load over Mike Mewett's trees in Humpty Doo?   Picture: ELISE DERWIN

CROCS IN THE
CABINET

THE Territory is semi-obsessed by politics and our readers, while they don't like to admit it, love the game and how we report it. Sometimes, though, we can get ourselves in trouble. When we called North Korean dictator Kim Jong-un a KIM-BECILE on the front page some readers were concerned we had put the Territory's security at risk.

The rise of the United States President Donald Trump has also led us to some fantastic front pages and homegrown Territory politics continues to throw up some cracking stories and headlines.

And we used to think we had the crazy politicians thing all to ourselves, but recent hijinks in Canberra are giving our Territorian pollies a run for their money.

TERRITORY TOP 10 IN WORLD FOR INVESTMENT ATTRACTIVENESS

NT Business REVIEW

$1 billion Berrimah development ready

NT BUSINESS REVIEW >> STARTS P13

STRANDED TREKKER RESCUED AFTER ORDEAL

REPORT >> P7

Wednesday, November 9, 2016   ntnews.com.au $1.40 Country freight 30 cents extra   Incl GST

NT News

YOUR VOICE IN THE TERRITORY

WE WANT YOU

Dear Americans,
Today you will likely have a new President of the United States.
No matter who wins, the nation is divided and it's time for you to move.
It's time you made your new home in the Northern Territory.
We have a lifestyle unmatched anywhere else Down Under.
Even if you don't want to move here, it's time you came for a holiday.

D-DAY FOR THE DIVIDED STATES ⟩ **P4-5**

Disgruntled Yanks urged to move to NT

By Hayley Sorensen

NO matter the outcome of today's US election, tens of millions of Americans will be unhappy with their new president.

The traditional proclamation of Americans annoyed with an electoral result is to announce they're moving to Canada. But with population growth key to a healthy Northern Territory economy, unhappy American voters are being urged to head to the Territory instead.

Chief Minister Michael Gunner yesterday issued an invitation through the *NT News* to disenfranchised Americans to come Down Under.

"I grew up in Alice Springs with lots of Americans and I know they will bring a positive, friendly 'can do' spirit and get heavily involved at a grassroots level with community clubs," he said.

"Population growth means economic growth so having more Americans relocate to the Territory would be great for local business and create jobs." Mr Gunner said the Territory's first-rate food offerings should be enough to lure the notoriously hungry Americans to the Top End.

"We have the world's best laksas, premium mangoes and the mighty barramundi," he said. "The coffee is significantly better — including our iced coffee."

Mr Gunner said there were plenty of drawcards for Yanks.

"Our wildlife is incredible — and our crocs would eat their alligators," he said.

"We have an incredibly multicultural, multi-faith and harmonious community."

The welcome would even be extended to Trump fans, should Americans have the sense to not elect the wall-loving, billionaire real estate mogul-turned human Cheezel.

"Everyone deserves a second chance," he said of Trump supporters. "There is no better place to discover the benefits of a diverse and vibrant community than the Territory."

Though polling may show Hillary Clinton is on track to hand her opponent a shellacking, odds significantly shortened for a Trump victory yesterday when Hank the American alligator chose the reality star as the likely winner.

Hank, who lives at Crocodylus Park, was presented with pictures of Mr Trump and Mrs Clinton and encouraged to take a snap at the candidate he believed would be the next US president. Like many of his fellow Americans, the reptile appeared unenamoured of both options. After several minutes of indecision, Hank chowed down on the hunk of meat attached to the picture of Mr Trump.

Hank is originally from Florida, the southern state known for retirees, guns and conservatism.

With overarching responsibility of US defence strategy, the next Commander-in-Chief will have a big local impact on the NT.

Barack Obama's plan to use Darwin as a base for the US military's pivot in Asia was finally locked in last month after a lengthy stoush over cost-sharing arrangements between the two nations. The agreements give some surety but a new president will have power to alter the course.

Hank the Alligator from Crocodylus Park chooses Donald Trump over Hillary Clinton to be the President of the United States Picture: HELEN ORR

NT News

YOUR VOICE IN THE TERRITORY

Friday, February 3, 2017   ntnews.com.au $1.40 Country freight 30 cents extra Incl GST

KIDDIES TRADE NUGGETS FOR SUSHI
NEW CRAZE >> P3

FUEL PRICES SURGE TO AMONG HIGHEST IN OZ
REPORT >> P7

BARBA'S SHOCK SWITCH TO UNION
>> SPORT

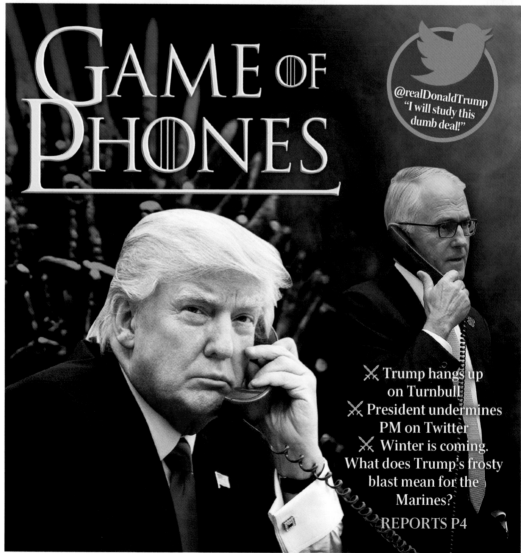

GAME OF PHONES

@realDonaldTrump
"I will study this dumb deal!"

⚔ Trump hangs up on Turnbull
⚔ President undermines PM on Twitter
⚔ Winter is coming. What does Trump's frosty blast mean for the Marines?

REPORTS P4

COPS ROLL OUT AUTOMATED TYRE SPIKES ON STREETS > P9

Turnbull made to look a fool

By Paul Toohey

THE day began with news that Malcolm Turnbull had donated $1.75m to his Liberal Party, leading to claims he "bought" the prime ministership. A manageable media problem for the PM and his office, but as we were sleeping, reporters from the *Washington Post* were knocking up a story that would quickly overtake it and bring into stark question Turnbull's trustworthiness.

The report directly contradicted Turnbull's claims of previous days that he had had a "constructive" talk with Trump on Sunday, whom he said was committed to honouring a deal to take 1250 asylum seekers and refugees from Nauru and Manus Island.

Trump knew that the deal — struck between Turnbull and the Obama Administration — presented a major domestic political problem, once US media saw the hypocrisies of Trump blockading visa holders from certain countries, including Iran, while letting in the offshore group, which is heavily populated by Iranians.

It appears Trump's team briefed the *Post* on the true nature of the conversation. Far from being collegiate, Trump was furious and insulting, yelling at Turnbull that it was "the worst deal ever" and the "worst call by far" he'd had speaking to leaders on Sunday. In essence, he said Australia was not facing up to its own problems.

Turnbull fronted the media, waving away questions about the report in the *Post*.

Perhaps, dumbstruck at Turnbull's denials, Trump launched a tweet designed to even further undermine Turnbull, whom he'd already left flapping meekly on a rock.

"I will study this dumb deal," Trump said, indicating it was far from sealed.

Trump has signalled the deal, which was always fraught, is all-but dead.

This won't kill ANZUS or anything so dire. But Trump has made Turnbull look like a fool.

A bad day for Turnbull. His worst day.

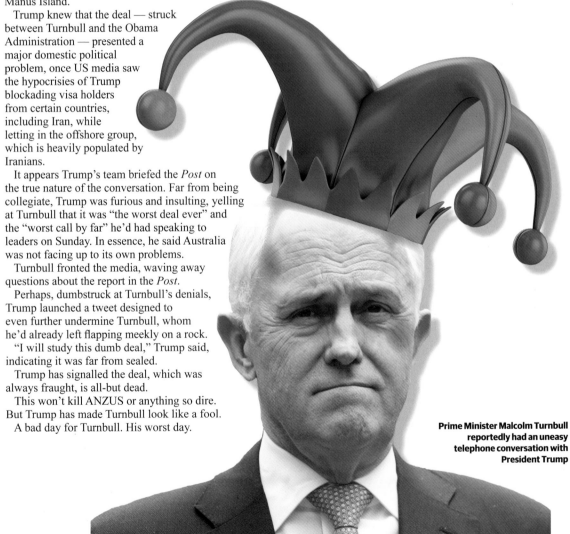

Prime Minister Malcolm Turnbull reportedly had an uneasy telephone conversation with President Trump

YOUR VOICE IN THE TERRITORY

NT News

Friday, January 6, 2017   ntnews.com.au $1.40 Country freight 30 cents extra Incl GST

FROM JAKARTA WITH HUFF

INDO ARMY CHIEF'S DARWIN SPY MISSION

picture digitally altered

EXCLUSIVE

General who suspended military ties claims he hired a tourist boat for recon in Darwin Harbour STORY >> P9

JAMES HIRD RUSHED TO HOSPITAL
DETAILS >> SPORT

SECOND ARREST IN HIT AND RUN CASE
REPORT >> P2

2016 OUR HOTTEST YEAR ON RECORD
STORY >> P3

Spying mission comes from Jakarta with huff

By Miles Godfrey, Jason Tin and Gary Shipway

THE diplomatic crisis between Australia and Indonesia has deepened after it emerged that Indonesia's top military boss — who accused Australia of recruiting Indonesian soldiers as spies — carried out a secret spy mission in Darwin.

Indonesia's armed forces chief Gatot Nurmantyo, the man who cut ties with Australia's military this week in a hissy fit over "offensive" materials at a Perth army school, carried out the weird amateur sleuthing trip around US military bases in the Top End. The touchy general recently accused Australia's top brass of recruiting Indonesia special forces troops as double agents. Defence Minister Marise Payne denied the allegations yesterday as she expressed regret for the training materials found in Perth and other "cultural" issues that have caused the spat.

"We certainly have indicated our regret that this has occurred and offence taken," she said.

General Nurmantyo boasted about his own spying exploits, outlining to a respected Indonesian media outlet how he recently went undercover to check out US marine facilities in Darwin.

"I went there pretending to be on a visit to Darwin and for one and half hours I hired a tourist boat," General Nurmantyo said. "I saw two [landing bases] had already been built. Even though Australia is a continental state — what does it need marines for?"

It remains unclear if General Nurmantyo, who is believed to harbour ambitions to one day become Indonesian president, enjoyed any other Darwin attractions, including a jumping crocodile cruise.

The Australian Defence Force said it was aware of reports in Indonesia about General Nurmantyo's trip. It remains unclear when the spying visit took place but Defence pointed out that General Nurmantyo was in Canberra and Sydney during October to meet with Chief of Defence Force Air Chief Marshal Mark Binskin.

Exercise Kakadu, a joint military air and sea exercise between Australia and our neighbouring countries, was held in late September prior to the General's October meetings.

The Indonesian general has previously criticised Australia's hosting of US marines and is widely viewed by academics as being less friendly towards Australia than former Indonesian military bosses.

"The new Indonesia chief of defence force equivalent is perhaps not as pro-Australian as some of his predecessors," said Australian Defence Association spokesman Neil James.

Indonesian President Joko Widodo played down the cutting off of military ties yesterday — and ordered General Nurmantyo to sort it out.

"Indonesia and Australia have agreed to respect each other, to appreciate each other and not interfere in each others' domestic affairs," he said.

General Gatot Nurmantyo said he took a tourist boat around Darwin to look at US Marine facilities
Picture: DONAL HUSNI / GETTY IMAGES

"We have already agreed on that and now I have ordered the minister of defence and the military chief to address the problem."

The report that General Nurmantyo claimed seeing US marine landing bases from a boat in Darwin Harbour had local officials scratching their heads as to where they could be. The belief is that General Nurmantyo was referring to the recently built barge ramp at East Arm, which any commercial business has access to. The East Arm barge ramp is a commercial facility funded by the Northern Territory Government and the Defence Department.

The barge ramp is not a military facility but provides Defence with logistics support and a strategic interface between land and sea for up to 60 days a year. For the remaining 300 days of the year, the facility is available for commercial use by private barge operators. Soldiers have trialled the ramp, loading tanks, trucks and plant equipment on to landing craft from HMAS *Adelaide*.

The previous CLP government made no secret of the ramp's development and conducted regular public bus tours to East Arm and the wharf precinct surrounds to herald their progress and the commercial opportunities being created for the port.

Wednesday, April 26, 2017   ntnews.com.au $1.40 Country height 30 cents extra Incl GST

NT News

YOUR VOICE IN THE TERRITORY

KIM-BECILE

North Korean media names Darwin as US nuclear war launch site >> P7

All your local news plus a tablet.

Conditions apply.

1800 031 353   ntnews.com.au/tablet

NT News

N Korea points finger at Darwin ...

By Gary Shipway

DARWIN is being used by North Korea as proof that the United States is preparing for nuclear war.

North Korea's Workers' Party's newspaper *Rodong Sinmun*, has accused America of "fanatically, crazily trying to optimise its nuclear war readiness" and claimed the deployment of 1250 US Marines in Darwin is an example of that.

"This is the largest scale US military presence in Australia after World War 2," the newspaper said.

The story was headlined: America prepares for nuclear war in different overseas military deployments.

The Australian Government has rejected the claims.

Defence Industry Minister Christopher Pyne said Australia wanted to avoid any military action with North Korea.

"We want the North Koreans to behave like reasonable international citizens – that means ending their missile testing and not preparing for a nuclear war with the US, Japan, South Korea and anyone else for that matter," he said.

The Darwin based air-strike force is led by Lieut. Colonel Brian Middleton who said the strategic importance of the US Marine deployment in Darwin is reflected in its size.

"I think that the commitment that we've taken to put a task force here with a conversation to get larger over the years says that we do think this is an important region," he said. "Being close to Southeast Asia and the Indian Ocean, the Indo Pacific position has always been important."

He pulled no punches when asked about the role the 1250-strong marine air ground task force deployment would play if tensions between his country and North Korea escalate into direct conflict.

"We stand ready to fight and win the night," he said. "The aviation combat element is our most robust deployment to Darwin."

There will be 13 aircraft, four tilt-rotor Ospreys, five Super Cobra helicopters and four Huey helicopters.

The marines are from 3rd Battalion, 4th Marine Regiment from Camp Pendleton, California. They will be based at Robertson Barracks, RAAF Base Darwin and Defence Establishment Berrimah.

The Northern Territory's Pine Gap military intelligence base just outside Alice Springs has also been touted as a possible target in the past.

Defence strategists for the time being have ruled this out. North Korea has worked on an intercontinental ballistic missile (ICBM) but has struggled with multistage rockets that could actually traverse the atmosphere at great distance.

Defence strategists have also questioned North Korea's guidance capacity over long range launches.

The top-secret Pine Gap military facility is important to US intelligence and military operations around the world. It plays a vital role in collecting a wide range of signals intelligence as well as providing information on early warning of ballistic missile launches.

Intelligence gathered here could be used to target nuclear weapons and is also used to support US and Japanese missile defence.

North Korean Supreme Leader Kim Jong-un

YOUR VOICE IN THE TERRITORY

NT News

THE NORTHERN TERRITORY PRESENTS

CROC ⓥⓢ UFO

ADAM GILES
CLP Reign Of Chaos

MICHAEL GUNNER
Untested Fiscal Operative

POLLING BOOTHS OPEN 8AM ★ CLOSE 6PM ★ TICKETS: FREE

★ COVERAGE >> PAGES 4-7

ELECTION NOTICE

VOTE TODAY
8:00 am to 6:00 pm
See pages 16 & 17 for your nearest voting centre

ntec.nt.gov.au | 1800 698 683

Voting is compulsory

2016 Territory Election

Got an opinion? Make it count.

Authorised by Iain Loganathan, Northern Territory Electoral Commission 80 Mitchell St, Darwin

Barbs traded on final day of long campaign

By Christopher Walsh

THE leaders of both major parties traded barbs on the final day of the election campaign yesterday.

Chief Minister Adam Giles wrote an open letter to all NT public servants claiming that a vote for Labor would mean a vote for losing their jobs.

Labor leader Michael Gunner joined over 50,000 other Territorians to cast his ballot early yesterday, declaring it time to "restore trust in government". Mr Giles, in his letter, said: "The future of the Northern Territory public service will be determined by how you vote," he wrote. "If Labor is owning up to sacking public servants before the election, imagine what nasty surprises are in store after the election."

Mr Gunner said after casting his vote: "When you vote early it's often because you know why you want to vote and I think a lot of Territorians at this election are keen for a new government."

Mr Gunner said he wouldn't be distracted by those types of "shenanigans" and reiterated Labor's pledge to find budget savings by cutting departments from 31 to 20. Cuts to staff would be limited to 11 chief executive positions and 15 deputy chief executives.

"Under Labor there will be no nasty surprises," he said.

Mr Giles also said yesterday that if his party is voted out of office the Territory would be plunged into a recession.

"We now need to knuckle down and manage our economy carefully," he told ABC radio. "If the Country Liberals are voted out on Saturday, the Territory will go into recession, there's no doubt about it."

Mr Gunner admitted there would be challenging economic times ahead.

"I'm not prepared to rush out and use the 'r' word — recession — yet. I think there are things that we can do to help the Territory economy," he said.

"The best way to stave off fears of a recession is by restoring confidence and there is nothing about the current term of government that gives confidence to people."

The NT Electoral Commission said yesterday that more than 38 per cent of registered voters had voted in early polls.

Those ballots will be counted tonight, along with the rest of the ballots expected to come in before polls close at 6pm. The NTEC also committed to having 80 per cent of all ballots counted by 8pm.

Mr Giles will spend election night in Alice Springs and Mr Gunner will be with the Labor team at the Waratahs Club.

Michael Gunner casts his early vote ahead of election day in Darwin while Chief Minister Adam Giles (inset) is back home in Alice Springs

OUR BIGGEST BINGO JACKPOT EVER

WIN $40,000
Details >> P14

SUNDAY Territorian

August 7, 2016 $1.50 Country freight 30c extra. Includes GST

TERRYMINATOR 2 JUDGMENT DAY

I'M BACK

EXCLUSIVE Mills set to run against CLP >> P4

Royal Flying Doctor Service

The RFDS Darwin Tourist Facility > Check out our

DIGITAL INTERACTIVE AD

on page **2**

HOLOGRAMS - VIRTUAL REALITY - WINDOW OF 1942 - RFDS PILATUS PC 12 AIRCRAFT

Mills expected to run against CLP in Blain

By Christopher Walsh

THE man Territorians elected as Chief Minister in 2012 is back and expected to announce he's running for his old seat of Blain — but this time as an independent, the *Sunday Territorian* can reveal.

Terry Mills, who was rolled as chief minister by Adam Giles seven months after the last election, told the *Sunday Territorian* yesterday he has renounced his CLP membership and slammed the Giles Government for its "unforgivable damage" to the Territory.

"After 20 years I have decided I can no longer remain a member of the CLP," Mr Mills said in an email. "It is a tragedy to see this once proud Territory party brought so low under the Giles Government.

"The last four years have done unforgivable damage to the Territory's national and international reputation. The CLP need to be held to account for putting its interests before those of the people of the Territory."

Mr Mills's announcement that he has forsaken the CLP is expected to send shock waves through the powerful Palmerston branch of the party, which is still divided over his ousting in 2013. Sources believe Mr Mills could announce as early as today that he will be seeking his former seat of Blain as an independent. He did not rule out contesting the seat in the statement, saying, "I will have more to say about this soon".

He added that he does not trust Labor to fix the problems currently facing the Territory.

"I have no confidence in the Labor Party's capacity to deal with the crime and anti-social behaviour that is a blight on so many communities," he said.

"Michael Gunner is simply not up to the challenge of repairing the immense damage of the Giles-Tollner administration."

An *NT News* commissioned poll last week indicated Mr Mills was much more popular than Adam Giles Territory-wide, with a net positive rating of 23 per cent compared to Mr Giles's net negative 32 per cent.

But it is unclear how that would translate to the Palmerston electorate of Blain.

Other polling numbers show the CLP losing their fortress of Palmerston in the August 27 election in a massive swing to Labor.

What effect Mr Mills's expected candidacy would have on the Palmerston seats is also unclear.

He was rolled by Mr Giles in March 2013, while overseas, in a party vote of 11–5.

Chief Minister Adam Giles and former Chief Minister Terry Mills after Mills announced his retirement in 2014
Picture: JUSTIN SANSON

SO... WHICH CREDIT CARD SHOULD WE USE NICOLE?

VISA
MASTER CARD
CHINA BANK
AMEX
DINERS CLUB
BANK CARD
ANZ

Illustration: STU THORNTON

HEY, BIG SPENDERS

* Govt to borrow $5.6 billion
* Manison: A budget of 'optimism'

$1.75 billion infrastructure spend
COVERAGE: P4-7 & NT Biz Review

New Kmart Coolalinga opens today from 8am.
Coolalinga Central

Spending to get NT out of hole: Manison

First budget lacking vision

Analysis by Christopher Walsh

THE Gunner Government's first Budget was as scary as predicted, with record levels of deficits, debts and borrowing with very little in the way of reforms for the future. The Government is facing a number of depressing economic conditions but did not show yesterday they were planning for the future.

The Treasurer's line about it being a Budget "for optimists not pessimists" was worrying.

Territorians deserve a Budget for realists.

This is a short-term Budget that was not designed with the type of foresight for the types of reforms needed to wean the NT off its GST addiction. Its focus was on sustaining jobs and investing in infrastructure for the here and now through racking up debt.

Ms Manison said the only way to plan for the future was "to grow the economy" but failed to explain the Government's plan to do that long term. Artificially propping up the Territory's economy is not sustainable, especially without a proper population strategy in place.

Without a firm plan for the future, the Territory is not in a good place. Waiting to see if this massive spend gets us out of the economic doldrums is not a plan. All debts are payable sooner or later and interest payments projected to cost $1 million a day is certainly not sustainable.

CDU associate professor of economics Ram Vemuri said that simply looking at the future as an optimist is not pragmatic. "It needs to be looked at in more ways than simple optimism," he said.

"Is building an optimistic future for the NT possible without changing the way the budget addresses things? More of the same underpins this budget.

"Yes, we need expenditure in a downturn but we need to think about budgets beyond external stimulus.

"What happens when these expenditures dry up? Jobs disappear and people leave. We need to break the cycle through budget expenditures. An opportunity was lost for a fundamental shift."

The Government's Budget slogan was "investing for the future". But Labor lost the chance yesterday to show they recognise there is a future and to plan for it accordingly.

$6.7 billion total budget

$1.3 billion deficit

$18 million for a PET scanner and cyclotron

$27 million to run the royal commission

$2.5 million for a hydrotherapy pool at Palmerston Hospital

$4.26 billion in Commonwealth funding

$225 million in mining and petroleum revenue

$1 million in interest payments a day on that debt

$4.57 million for aged care services

$60 extra to register a four-wheel drive

$5.4 billion of debt by 2020/21

$77.88 million to upgrade the Arnhem Hwy

$36 million over two years to commission the new Palmerston Hospital

$2 million on CCTV

$75 million for essential services in indigenous communities

NOT JUST FULL
OF CROC

WHILE we love to have a laugh in the *NT News* office we don't ever turn away from the important stories that need to be told. When a two-year-old girl was abused in Tennant Creek, we launched a relentless campaign called Save Our Children; which implored governments of all levels to act. Our award-winning campaign led to then Prime Minister Malcolm Turnbull visiting Tennant Creek — only the second PM in history to go to the troubled town. We were also the first newspaper in Australia to vouch for same-sex marriage on our front page. That front page was so successful it reached 2.8 million people alone through our Facebook and Twitter channels.

We are proud we aren't just full of croc — just like Territorians, when something is going wrong, we are going to point it out.

V8 CONVOY TURNS HEADS
STORY , PICS >> P8-9

ULTIMATE WHAT'S ON GUIDE
ENTERTAINMENT >> P36-37

8-PAGE WORLD CUP LIFTOUT
>> INSIDE

WORLD CUP
DARING TO DREAM
CAHILL AND SOCCEROOS ARE READY

Thursday, June 14, 2018 — ntnews.com.au — $1.60 Country People 30 cents extra Incl GST

We're for *you*
YOUR V...

NT News

SAVE OUR CHILDREN

Prime Minister Malcolm Turnbull in Canberra yesterday Picture: KYM SMITH

It's been four months since the rape of a two-year-old girl sparked a national crisis and nine months since he set foot inside the Territory. This missing-in-action Prime Minister for the East Coast has shown he ...

SIMPLY DOES NOT CARE

FULL REPORT >> P7   EDITORIAL >> P14

CrownBet DARWIN TRIPLE CROWN 15 – 17 JUNE 2018

TODAY from 10am
DRIVERS SIGNING & SHOWTIME FMX SHOW
Meet the 2018 Supercar drivers at Raintree Park and experience daredevil stunts from the ShowTime FMX team

5:45PM SUNSET DRIVERS SIGNING ON THE BEACH
Plus Fox Sports Inside Supercars broadcasting live from Mindil Beach Sunset Markets

DCWRA   CITY OF DARWIN   WWW.DARWINSUPERCARS.COM.AU

MEET THE RED BULL HOLDEN RACING TEAM 7PM @ KERRY HOLDEN

WIN TICKETS TO DISNEY PRINCESS FILM FESTIVAL

DETAILS >> P8

JOANNE LEES RECOUNTS OUTBACK HORROR

STORY >> P3

MISCHIEF AND MAYHEM JUST $2.60 TODAY ONLY

COUPON >> P6

ROALD DAHL MISCHIEF AND MAYHEM

Monday, February 13, 2017 · · · ntnews.com.au · · · $1.40 Country freight 20 cents extra Incl GST

NT News

YOUR VOICE IN THE TERRITORY

NORTHERN TERRITORY

PERTH

ADELAIDE

BRISBANE

CANBERRA

SYDNEY

MELBOURNE

HOBART

Hey Sco-Mo, you've been Treasurer for 17 months now and you haven't visited us. When are we going to....

SEE YOU IN THE NT?

STORY > P2   EDITORIAL > P12

YOUR VOICE IN THE TERRITORY

NT News

Wednesday, July 27, 2016   ntnews.com.au $1.40 Country freight 30 cents extra Incl GST

Eleven months ago, the Children's Commissioner handed the Territory Government a report detailing systemic abuse of young prisoners in detention.

The report was built around the very same videos that aired on national TV on Monday night.

The Government ignored the report and even pushed for tougher measures.

They only acted yesterday following national and international outrage.

John Elferink was sacked as Corrections Minister but still remains Attorney-General and Children and Families Minister.

Now, many around Australia are saying ...

SACK THE LOT OF THEM

FULL COVERAGE >> PAGES 4-11

The image that shocked a nation

By Hayley Sorensen

DYLAN Voller — the hooded face of the Territory's child prisoner shame — was a little kid with a big mouth.

Childhood trauma compounded behavioural issues and ADHD. He was difficult to control, and that big mouth saw him in and out of detention since he was 11.

His offending escalated and now 18, Dylan is serving out the final few weeks of a 20-month sentence in an adult prison for an ice binge during which he tried to run over a police officer in Alice Springs.

"His mouth was his weapon, because he's tiny," his sister Kirra told the *NT News*.

A 17-year-old Dylan Voller sits shackled to a chair by his ankles, wrists and head, a hood obscuring his face   Picture: ABC/FOUR CORNERS

"He's always been a little boy and he's never had a father figure. He's always been lost, looking for that role model."

Pictures chronicling Voller's abuse at the hands of the NT justice system have shocked Australia. The vision, first aired on *Four Corners*, showed Dylan, then 13, slammed to a mattress on the floor by a prison guard. Footage of other incidents show Dylan growing up with institutional abuse the only constant in his life.

In the final frames, a 17-year-old Voller sits eerily still, shackled to a chair by his ankles, wrists and head, a hood obscuring his face.

Kirra said she found the footage difficult to watch.

"I wanted to turn the TV off," she said. "The minute it started, I couldn't watch it. But I needed to watch it because I needed to know what my brother had been through so I could be there for him." She said she was overwhelmed and humbled by the support from all over Australia and welcomed the news of a royal commission, but said it would mean little to her brother in practical terms. "It won't do anything for him. He's not even in Don Dale anymore, he's 19 this year; he's in an adult jail. It's not going to help him so it doesn't really mean anything to me at all," she said.

But Kirra said it was sweet to finally be vindicated in her belief that what happened to her brother was wrong.

"We thought for so long it was wrong," she said. "But everybody else is saying 'no, it's right' and you start to think 'OK, maybe it's right'.

"But after seeing the response, it's not right at all."

Dylan is eligible for release next month. It will be the first time he will exist in the real world as an adult. He has a job lined up in Humpty Doo but with NT recidivism rates the worst in the country, the odds are stacked against him. Kirra said Dylan was robbed of a childhood by the NT justice system. "He's just a lost little boy on the inside who needed guidance and love and support but from the age of 10 he was isolated and separated from everyone and everything rather than being built up into that person he was supposed to be," she said.

Despite everything he has endured, Kirra said Dylan still had a chance to build himself a life, and was optimistic about his future. "Anyone who saw the footage wouldn't have thought he was that boy in the video," she said. "He tries to be funny and smile and laugh things off for the sake of everybody else around him. I think that personality trait will help him get through."

Front pages showing how the *NT News* covered the issue

NT News

YOUR VOICE IN THE TERRITORY

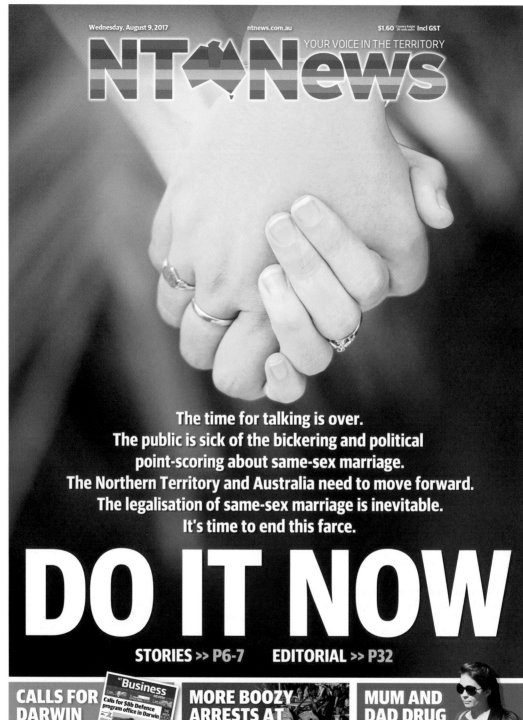

The time for talking is over.
The public is sick of the bickering and political
point-scoring about same-sex marriage.
The Northern Territory and Australia need to move forward.
The legalisation of same-sex marriage is inevitable.
It's time to end this farce.

DO IT NOW

STORIES >> P6-7　　　EDITORIAL >> P32

CALLS FOR DARWIN DEFENCE OFFICE

NT BUSINESS REVIEW

Calls for $8b Defence program office in Darwin

MORE BOOZY ARRESTS AT DARWIN CUP CARNIVAL

PICTURES >> P5

MUM AND DAD DRUG DEALERS LOCKED UP

STORY >> P2

Front page goes viral

By Hayley Sorensen

YESTERDAY'S historic front page of the *NT News*, which urged our pollies to act on same-sex marriage, is believed to have become the most retweeted front page in Australian history.

It is estimated that through Twitter and Facebook it was seen by up to 2 million people.

The record-breaking front page comes as the Senate yesterday blocked the Government's bid to pass laws to enable a compulsory vote, meaning Australians will instead vote in a voluntary postal plebiscite run by the Australian Bureau of Statistics.

It has sparked fears Territorians living in remote areas without access to the postal system may be shut out.

NT Labor Senator Malarndirri McCarthy said Territorians without access to mail would have no voice in the "clearly discriminatory" poll.

"Thousands of Territorians living in dwellings without letterboxes or personal postboxes will be excluded from voting," she said. "There has been no effort by the Government to address the logistical needs of the residents of town camps, remote indigenous communities and homelands in the NT who, under this proposal, will not have their views heard. They are being effectively silenced."

Finance Minister Mathias Cormann's office did not respond to questions from the *NT News* yesterday as to how those living in remote communities would be counted.

It's estimated the plebiscite will cost $122 million. But there are concerns the ABS won't be able to handle the workload.

Public sector union deputy secretary Melissa Donnelly said the agency was already under pressure.

More than 160 ABS staff have lost their jobs in the past nine months. Ballot papers will hit mailboxes from September 12 and the final result is expected by November 15.

A High Court challenge, initiated by independent Andrew Wilkie, is in the works on the grounds there are constitutional problems with the Government paying for the poll without the approval of Parliament.

The *NT News*' front page yesterday, which featured a rainbow masthead and a call to end the farce and legislate for same-sex-marriage through the Parliament quickly, went viral on social media.

It attracted attention from other media outlets and politicians and prompted former CLP leader Jodeen Carney to tell ABC Radio she was "appalled" at the conduct of the Coalition.

"If you are too afraid to cast your vote on the floor of the Parliament, you are in the wrong job," she said.

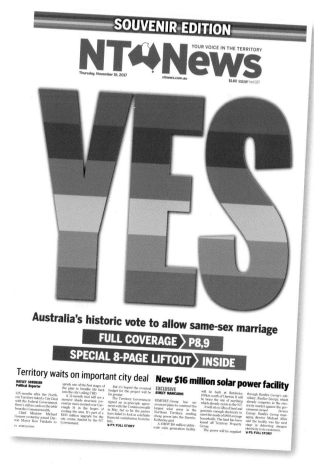

The *NT News* front page from 16 November 2017 celebrating the outcome of the same sex marriage postal vote where almost 60% of Aussies who participated voted 'yes' to same sex mariage equality

EXTRA
EXTRA

WE are really proud that our front pages are getting rock star attention. It is very cool that Territorians, Southerners and foreigners are united in their chuckles. For every laugh we get, every click or social media share, we feel like the *NT NEWS* is helping make the world a happier place. But, there is one side of the paper that only Territorians get to see most of the time — our street posters. At the risk of bragging, we are going to brag. They are short, sharp and to the point. They are, not to make an English teacher's eyes roll too much, poetry. Well, almost!

NT News *YOUR VOICE IN THE TERRITORY*
SATURDAY, JULY 2, 2016

HORSE IN LOVE WITH GOAT

... AND NOT MUCH ELSE HAPPENING TODAY

NT News *YOUR VOICE IN THE TERRITORY*
TUESDAY, OCTOBER 18, 2016

CRAZY CLOWN ARRESTED AT MACCA'S

NT News *YOUR VOICE IN THE TERRITORY*
FRIDAY, JULY 22, 2016

HOW MY DENTURES MELTED IN BUFFET TOASTER

NT News *YOUR VOICE IN THE TERRITORY*
SATURDAY, AUGUST 13, 2016

WHY GEN Y WON'T CLEAN DUNNIES

NT News *YOUR VOICE IN THE TERRITORY*
THURSDAY, AUGUST 18, 2016

FREAKY FISH CAUGHT IN NT WATERS

NT News *YOUR VOICE IN THE TERRITORY*
TUESDAY, AUGUST 30, 2016

CHEEKY BUGGER TOOK MY PLUGGERS

NT News *YOUR VOICE IN THE TERRITORY*
WEDNESDAY, AUGUST 31, 2016

NT HAS NATION'S RUDEST PLACE NAMES

NT News *YOUR VOICE IN THE TERRITORY*
TUESDAY, OCTOBER 4, 2016

FISHOS TURN INTO PRAWN STARS

NT News — *YOUR VOICE IN THE TERRITORY*
THURSDAY, OCTOBER 13, 2016

AIR FORCE IGNORES UFOs IN SKIES

NT News — *YOUR VOICE IN THE TERRITORY*
TUESDAY, NOVEMBER 15, 2016

NUDE RUDE DUDE RUNS AMOK

NT News — *YOUR VOICE IN THE TERRITORY*
WEDNESDAY, NOVEMBER 16, 2016

NAKED COUPLE CAUGHT IN SEX ROMP

SUNDAY Territorian
NOVEMBER 20, 2016

BE AFRAID! SUPER TOADS ARE EVOLVING

NT News — *YOUR VOICE IN THE TERRITORY*
TUESDAY, NOVEMBER 22, 2016

MAN HOOKED IN HEAD BY OWN LURE

NT News — *YOUR VOICE IN THE TERRITORY*
MONDAY, NOVEMBER 28, 2016

HORNY MANGO FOUND IN TOP END

NT News — *YOUR VOICE IN THE TERRITORY*
WEDNESDAY, DECEMBER 7, 2016

ALIENS BLAMED FOR MANGO HEIST

SUNDAY Territorian
JANUARY 22, 2017

BARE-BUM THIEF LEAVES SURPRISE IN THE LOO

NT News — *YOUR VOICE IN THE TERRITORY*
FRIDAY, JANUARY 27, 2017

DOGS IN LOVE WITH HOT PET PIG

NT News *YOUR VOICE IN THE TERRITORY*
FRIDAY, JANUARY 12, 2010

MAN BASHED BY PRAWN

NT News *YOUR VOICE IN THE TERRITORY*
FRIDAY, DECEMBER 5, 2008

MOTORISTS AMAZING STORY

'PACK OF DOGS ATE MY CAR'

NT News *YOUR VOICE IN THE TERRITORY*
FRIDAY, JULY 14, 2014

DEAD WOMAN TOLD TO MOW HER LAWN

NT News *YOUR VOICE IN THE TERRITORY*
THURSDAY, MAY 20, 2010

CROC STALKS NUDIST BEACH

NT News *YOUR VOICE IN THE TERRITORY*
MODAY, NOVEMBER 11, 2013

VOMITING MAN STUCK TO WINDSCREEN

40 BIKIES ARRESTED

NT News *YOUR VOICE IN THE TERRITORY*
FRIDAY, MARCH 12, 2014

PLAN TO STOP COWS FARTING

NT News *YOUR VOICE IN THE TERRITORY*
FRIDAY, JULY 22, 2011

SHAGGIN' IN THE PADDY WAGON

NT News *YOUR VOICE IN THE TERRITORY*
SATURDAY, NOVEMBER 20, 2010

HORNY LIZARD NEEDS A ROOT